MW01173684

Unseal Your

Best Life

POEMS REVEALING PAST, PRESENT, AND PERFECT MOMENTS

Compiled by **The Unsealed**
Contributing Writers:

Abigail Stopka, Afton Villanueva, Aimee Concepcion, Ala, Alessandra Suchodolski, Alexcia Cegelski, Alexis King, Alexis McWhorter, Ali Mazza, Amanda Ann, Anastasia Quintanilla, Antoinette Gonzalez, Antonieta Paco, Ariana Manley, Ash Raymond James, Ashley Graham, Astrida Hara, Aubrey Schuring, Autumn Harrington, Bre Mcilroy, Camerial Kristen, Cherie, Chloe, Christine Navarrete, Christina Wilder, Chrys Takashige, Crystal Mulligan, Cyantha Key, Danéa Summerford, Danielle Patino, Darlene Cervantes, Destinee Ramos, Dominic Valim, Dominique Nesbitt, Dr. Cortnie S. Baity, Drew Zuhosky, Emily Warner, Este Masters, Famo Musa, Flannery Joyce, Gabrielle Postlethwaite, Gerald Washington, Giselle Moran, Grace Catan, Grayson Bell, Hanna Gootée, Hannah Gonneville, Hannah Gray, Hirasoul, Isabella Riesco, Jacqueline Sonia, Jake April, Jamell Crouthers, Jane P., Janet Joshua, Janet Banks, Jaselynn Villalpando, Jennifer St.Clair (J.ST.C.), Jody Seymour, Johanna Deletti, Jonathan Odle, Jovon Reed, Julia McCarty, Julianna Waldvogel, K. S. Love, Kalianah Wogoman, Karen Rice, Karina Rodriguez, Karissa Howden, Kelly Lieberman, Kelsea Guckin, Kevya Sims, Kortney R. Garwood, LaShae Eaddy, Leah Joy, Leyla Jordan, Liz Medina, Lore X, Lorinda Boyer, Lynn Humphreys, Maggie Faye, Mel Taul, Melanie A. Greene, Melissa Rodriguez, Michael Delianides, Michelle, Morgan Bland, Mz.EYG Queen Era, Naiya Figueroa, Necia Campbell, Nicole Hughes, Nicole Kisslinger, Nysha Lee, Oswald Perez, Phoenix Ríszing, Poetry Veguez, Pretty Dee, Rachel Brennan, Raphael Inoa, Rashan Speller, Raven Wallace, Ray Whitaker, Rayven Washington, Rebecca Engle, Ricardo Albertorio, Rick Writes, Roses, Sarah Ludlum, Sarah Perez, Sherry Noble, Sofia Armstrong, Sole Love, Sun Rose, Sydnee Cabrera, Sylvia St.Martin, Tamara Gallagher, Tasha Uliano, Tiara Smith, Tracy Barnes, Vee, Vicki Trusselli, Victoria Atterberry, Vision Woodall, Zinamene Emue

Copyright © 2024 by Lauren Brill Media LLC
All rights reserved.

No part of this publication may be reproduced, distributed, or transmitted in any form or by any means, including photocopying, recording, or other electronic or mechanical methods, without the prior written permission of the publisher, except as permitted by U.S. copyright law. However, contributors maintain ownership rights of their individual poems and as such retain all rights to publish and republish their work.

Book Cover by Marija Džafo
Layout Design by Marija Džafo

2024

ISBN Paperback: 979-8-9904346-1-5
ISBN Ebook: 979-8-9904346-2-2

CONTENT GUIDANCE:
This book contains adult
content and language that
may be triggering for some.
Please read with care.

What is The Unsealed?

The Unsealed (**theunsealed.com**) is a writing community where people write, share, and respond to personal and inspirational open letters. We hold weekly events and conversations, inviting interesting guests to talk to our community about their stories. Our platform aims to heal, empower, connect, encourage, and inspire people to persevere through their problems.

All the stories and poems in this book are written by members of The Unsealed community. Our writers are people of various backgrounds, ages, and writing levels. The purpose of this books is to amplify, connect, and celebrate the diverse voices within our community.

If you would like to message someone in this book or read more of their writing, you can plug their username into this url: https://theunsealed.com/members/username/

Dedication

We dedicate this book to anyone who feels time is moving too slowly. May this book remind you of the special moments in your past, present, and future.

Contents

GOALS FOR THE NEW YEAR 111

UNSEAL YOUR
BEST LIFE

POEMS
REVEALING
PAST,
PRESENT,
AND PERFECT
MOMENTS

Introduction

Dear Unsealers,

When I was a kid, at the end of every school year, I was always amazed by how fast the time passed. But then I would think about the year through the lens of repeating it all over again. The mere thought felt overwhelming and exhausting, and suddenly, that same school year felt much slower.

So how can the same time period feel so fast and so slow depending on the vantage point?

I have endured many challenges and worked through various roadblocks throughout my life. In fourth grade, some girls in my class weren't so nice to me, leaving mean messages on my answering machine and giggling while they stared at me and whispered. At the time, it was so hurtful. In high school, two strangers sexually assaulted me, and I didn't know how to process or face the reality of what those two boys did to me. After college, I got engaged but wasn't ready to get married, and navigating such a big decision with another person's feelings on the line was confusing and heartbreaking (to say the least). And throughout my tenure as a sportscaster, bosses, co-workers, and other people in the industry mistreated me more times than I can recount.

With all that said, there were so many memorable moments between those hardships — moments of excitement, kindness, and fulfilling accomplishments that I will remember for the rest of my life. In fourth grade, those mean girls squeezed me out of their lunch table, but my friend Patrice not only stuck up for me but left that table to eat beside me. In high school, while I struggled to process my assault, I also had so many fun nights with my friends, like memorizing songs and exchanging secrets in my basement with my ride or die, Tonia. Countless times, we laughed till our bellies hurt and danced until our feet blistered. After I broke off my engagement, as hard as it was, I started rollerblading every day and taking aimless long walks around midtown Manhattan, relaxing, processing my thoughts, and finding my peace. As a sports reporter, I have interviewed and met some of the greats: Michael Jordan, Billie Jean King, LeBron James, and Muhammed Ali (to name a few). I covered a World Series, and multiple NBA Finals and NBA Drafts. In 2008, my job during the NBA Draft week was to follow around the likely number one pick, Derrick Rose, and write what it was like to be a top pick. My boss's boss's boss asked me how my night was going toward the end of the draft.

I responded with a huge smile, "Would it be unprofessional to tell you that this might be the best night of my life?"

And nothing, and I mean nothing, can compare to the day I called my dad hysterically crying midday in a stairwell at my job on Long Island when I was 23 years old to tell him that the National Academy of Television Arts and Sciences nominated me for four Emmy awards in the largest television market in the country.

What I have come to realize is that it's our challenges that slow life down, but the moments in between that speed time up. While those tough experiences taught me invaluable lessons and shaped who I am, I don't want to be in fourth grade again. I don't want to go through the hurdles I faced in high school again. I don't want to endure another serious breakup. And I certainly don't want to be harassed and mistreated while pursuing my job like I was for so many years. With that said, I wish I could lean into the joy of those fun times just a little bit harder. I still want to celebrate all the days that I achieved a goal of mine despite whatever tried to stand in my way. And I would love to feel, even just for one more second, the excitement from the different explorations I went on and experiences I was lucky enough to have during periods when life was a bit more carefree.

Philosopher Ralph Waldo Emerson said, "It's not the destination, it's the journey."

However, I believe life is just as much, if not more, about the little moments regardless of their significance in your life's story.

I asked you, members of The Unsealed community, to share your favorite moment of last year, your goals for this year, and your idea of a perfect day. In this book, I included many of your stories, regardless of your writing level or perspective. I hope that doing so helps you celebrate, feel, and acknowledge the moments that make life a beautiful adventure, no matter how fast or slow yours seems to be moving right now.

With love, hope, and faith,

Lauren Brill

BEST DAY OF 2023

By Rebecca Engle
Username: rengle3

———————

Graduatedism

On the day I graduated a lone star shone brightly
With honors and triumph that seemed unlikely.
In the face of discrimination, I held my head high
As I alone embraced this achievement with pride.

While others graduated without any strife
I battled biases throughout my life.
My strength, hidden behind Autism's veil,
A power within that could never fail.

Being the recipient of such a grade
I earned this distinction despite the parade
Of doubts and prejudices that tried to sway
Yet undeterred I persevered every single day.

Their paths were free from disdain
While I wrestled with enduring pain.
Magna cum laude, a crown
Worn amidst discrimination's critique.

This special day of mine shines bright and true
Born from struggles they couldn't view.
May it stand tall as a testament clear
To resilience against odds.

Rebecca Engle

By Lorinda Boyer
Username: lorinda

——————————

2023

So much happened to me
In this year of twenty, twenty-three.
I got new hips for which to run
Each morning, each day, rain, or sun.
An essay of mine was published in a book.
I'm still quite sure I don't like to cook.
My father's progressed illness made me see
How unbelievably fragile this life can be.
Miss Mollie my sweet yorkie-poo
Turned six, in dog years, forty-two.
I ran in many races at varying paces.
And made friends with people from faraway places.

But the absolute best part of twenty, twenty-three
Was celebrating ten years with my wife, Sandy.

Lorinda Boyer

By Isabella Riesco
Username: isabellar

———————

Year Of The Rabbit

2023 was the year of the rabbit, the year to break habits, no longer deal with havoc.

Symbolizing peace and prosperity, a time to seize the opportunities and highlight our original rarities.

My year was a year of change, a year of vision, and a year of great decisions.

Although there are so many memorable moments, the most fond would be the day I changed perspectives.

I woke up one morning no longer in a mind that felt hazed, it was clear as day, I needed to change my pace.

I longed for independence and self-sufficiency, dealing with my inconsistency was no longer my consistency.

I explored my passions with the arts.
I will never forget the day I was accepted to exhibit my work at the tall building called City Hall.
I was over the moon, so far beyond what I ever thought I could become.

33

The same year I also took a leap and started my own business.
Past me was there to bear witness to my accomplishments in astonishment.

The joys I felt from a simple shift in mind, how divine to finally get rid of my mental decline, which realigned my dopamine to an all new high.

As the theory of numerology states, the number 23 symbolizes manifestation.

I believe our greatest form of manifestation is to eliminate all our frustrations, and self-preservations, and turn them into our future elevation.

My best moment of 2023 was that of reincarnation.

My 2024 will be of curation between all my new dreams, beliefs, and creations.

Isabella Riesco

By Pretty Dee
Username: bakerdeandrea94@icloud.com

———————————

Anyways, Life Is Good... Gooder Than Good

To my Unsealed family,

Every day is a favorite day for me
I opened my eyes this morning and I could see
I could move my legs and stand on my feet
Wiggle my toes
And touch my nose
Use my mind to write this prose

Running water, working lights
Food in my fridge
Roof over my head
Despite my many obstacles
I am not dead.

I can put a smile on my face
Even in the darkest place
Because every day I breathe
is my favorite day

I remember the days
when I didn't think this way
I remember wanting to hide
And wish the world away

I thought the only way
I could find peace
Is if I was laid in a linen-lined box
And placed in a plot
While the words
"With deepest sympathy"
Are recited to my kids and family
And I be laid to rest
"In loving memory"
Yes, every day is my favorite day

Even when it didn't go as planned
And even the days I was
Surrounded by my enemies
And outmanned

Through every experience this year
I have learned life is grand
And to push away all fear
And run full speed ahead
I dare myself to stay the course
And in every moment, minute, hour
Day and season
That my breath is more than
Enough reason
To let every day be my favorite
Even on the bad days I will claim it
You will never grow
If the sun is always shining
And the sky is never raining
This year I learned how to
Not only love the rain,
But dance in it
Every day is my favorite day
Because the breath in my body means I am winning.

Peace and Love,

Dee

By Karissa Howden
Username: karissahowden

Simple Days

Lifting weights first thing
I just love the feeling it brings.
I learned a new skill,
rolling cappelletti
What a calming thrill.
Two hours lead me
directly to a nap.
Upon rising,
We packed the car and
grabbed the lil chap
Headed out for dinner surrounded by the sap.
Nothing but trees, him, you and I.
Can't forget the calming night sky.
The grilled burgers were delicious

Hungry bears would've been vicious.
Loved this day,
The work, the chill.
Time to finish it off with a hot shower and
clock in for a quick croissant drill.
Back at it in the morning
I don't care
A life like this keeps me from scorning.

Karissa Howden

By Janet Banks
Username: janetbanks

"Weeping May Endure For A Night But Joy Cometh In The Morning."

25 December 2023
Christmas Day

"Weeping may endure for a night
But joy cometh in the morning."

Psalm 30:5

My Dearest Sean:

As I was reading our friend Lauren Brill's website, the community was invited to reflect upon and write a letter about our favorite day of 2023. Sounds easy, right? Sometimes, as we enter the holy season of Christmas each year, we often reflect on the totality of the year. However, as a grieving mother, I found myself a bit challenged to write this missive as just 18 months, 13 days ago, you left this earth and transcended through the clouds, the galaxies, and the stars and onto God's Paradise. It almost feels like a betrayal to feel joy but the reading of Psalm 30:5 lifts our spirit to do otherwise.

After much reflection, I chose Wednesday, 23 August as the day and date as the single day that brought much joy and therefore my favorite day of 2023. This summer day was the selected day that the inaugural Sean Scott Strother Memorial Scholarship Fundraiser was held. The scholarship was created in loving memory of you as a beloved son and amazing father. Additionally, you were such a "teckie" and enjoyed all that technology had to offer and that was manifested in your home life, your professional career as a software solutions engineer, and in your extracurricular activities, including using technology to track biking with GPS. So it was apropos that we had envisioned a bright future for young scholars who plan to pursue a career in the Science, Technology, Engineering, Arts and Mathematics (STEAM) field, with College Now Greater Cleveland Inc. managing the fund.

The event committee consisted of members of your family and dear friends. We had methodically and meticulously planned out all of the details for an outside event on The

Bluff at a venue along the breathtaking shores of Cleveland's beautiful Lake Erie! We were ecstatic!

Thumbs up! The day prior to the event, we checked the weather forecast and had expected good weather on Wednesday. However, on the day of the event, we woke up to gray skies and gentle rain which progressively became worse. There was significant flash flooding and thunderstorms and the hardest hit areas were along the lakeshore, with five to seven inches of rainfall. You know what I was thinking—that the expected guest list of 50-plus would begin to diminish.

Good news! As we entered the venue, a young server introduced himself to me and shared an inspiring word.

He said, "Is this your event?" I answered affirmatively, apparently with a look of pensiveness.

The server continued, "Don't worry. Your event will be just fine! And, we'll have a bit of sunshine."

Unbeknownst to me, the venue staff had transformed the mansion to accommodate my event to a glorious indoor event! With that, guests who were not deterred by the ferocious storms, gray skies, and flooding began to trickle in. Close to 80 individuals joined us—family, friends, colleagues, and your BFFs. Miraculously, at one point during the event, like magic, the sun was shining which afforded our special guests to venture out of the mansion and onto The Bluff overlooking the picture-perfect Lake Erie. I believe that there was divine intervention. What do you think?

The fundraiser was awesome and successful! Every single one of your amazing friends, colleagues, family, new friends as well as event staff contributed to the success of this event! They showed up and showed out! Your closest friends created the most amazing silent auction baskets, lovingly entitled "Sean's Favorite Things." These unique baskets each reflected things that you enjoyed—Scotch, Date Night Basket, The Edible Art Experience Cookie Basket, Tech, Travel, Mobile Detailing, and a magnificent piece of art by a Cleveland artist.

The keynote speakers, all who knew you personally, shared remarkable stories about your kind attributes, your education at Cuyahoga Community College and its impact on your career and weaved in the importance of education, technology, and the STEAM areas as it relates to the economic development of our community. Your unique gift of being able to meet people where they are and go from "the mailroom to the boardroom" was just as important as your technology education.

We raised over \$17K which was 59% over plan. As a result of such a successful fundraiser, in 2024, we will be able to offer a selected scholar from the Cleveland Now Strother Scholarship Fund a renewable annual scholarship!

August 23 was indeed my favorite day!

Sean, your influence is enduring as well as impactful.

I love you dearly and you are missed immensely.

All my Love,
Mom

Janet Banks

By Tracy Barnes
Username: poeticaddiction_365

———————————

Unexpected Love

Started the year manifesting love and success
I had my share of failed relationships
So finding love in 2023 came unexpectedly
Our first official date just so happened to fall
On my mom's death anniversary
What a hectic day
After my hair appointment
We went to the cemetery to visit my mom
How different that was
I've never taken anyone to visit my mom's grave
If my mom was alive
She would have so many questions
So it was only right
A dinner reservation at Carmine's

Because we both love Italian food
The rain couldn't put a damper on our mood
Even though my silk press became frizzy
We took pictures to capture the night
Along the Time Square bright lights
Honestly, that had to be the overall best day of 2023
As the month of June is often bittersweet to me
That day I forgot about the past pain that plagued my mind
Instead, I celebrated new beginnings
And toasted to a brand new love that would continue to shine!

Tracy Barnes

By Janet Joshua
Username: jjoshua

_____

Queridas Madres

Wow! You're a mom now, and you're 18 years old. Who would have thought that?

You just left high school and now you're getting ready to be a mom. How is that even possible?

When you're in high school, you have dreams of who you want to become as an adult. Being a mother at 18 wasn't the plan.

July 30, 1994, your first son was born. February 15, 2002, your second son was born. Two sons and they are both great bundles of joy.

The day comes and your son decides to get married. He gets engaged and you're so happy for him. Celebrating your child being engaged is totally different than actually seeing them get married.

Your son planned a wedding for May 2024 and decided last minute that he would have a small ceremony in City Hall beforehand. He calls to tell you he is getting married a little early.

Wow! Is this really happening? Your son is getting married. Your baby. He's getting married in 2023. Right now? Today? No way!

Watching your child grow for 25 years and then seeing him carry his dresser out into a moving truck to go on his own — the tears roll down your face. You wipe it with pride. You're okay.

The day comes and now he is walking down the aisle of City Hall to get married. The tears start to roll down your face again. Your son growing from a baby to a man in front of you daily is the best feeling ever. Tears of joy are inevitable.

He holds his soon-to-be wife's hand and begins to say his vows. You're looking and saying to yourself, "This is it; he's all grown up. He is not a baby anymore. How?"

He looks at her and says "I do". Tears rolled down again. It's all joy!

He's married. He's a man. He's on his own. It's now Mr. & Mrs. This is the best day of my year.

You have nothing to worry about because he's an amazing man, mature, loveable, ambitious, and resilient. Maybe you can put the mom guard down just a tiny bit. Relax your shoulders. Release!

49

Moms, I want you to know that motherhood has its ups and downs. It's not always going to be oxtails smothered in gravy with rice and beans. But it will be delicious. Just make sure you have a tall glass of liquid to wash it down with.

He's married. He's happy. He's smiling.

One of the biggest joys ever. I love you!

This is the best day ever! Congratulations Mr. & Mrs.

Janet Joshua

By Melanie A. Greene
Username: mel33x0

———————

Unexpected But Welcomed Growth

Dear friend,

Is your time up?

If you are a U.S. citizen like myself, it's that infamous letter in the mail. 'You have been summoned for jury duty.'

Once or twice I had to postpone it due to life: a wedding, being out of state and such. But this time, this time. It was time.

You know, it's so true that something happens when you least expect it.

I was called in for jury duty. The courthouse felt historic yet familiar. Those who weren't excused for one reason or another were called into the courtroom by the judge.

I remember entering the courtroom and the lights were bright. 'In God we trust' in silver letters behind the judge. All eyes on us—the defendant, the lawyer of the defendant, two prosecutors, several court officers and the stenographer—the 45 people moseying in the pews.

Then we learned about the case from the judge. It was a criminal larceny case and the defendant was a young adult, 26.

Before we knew it, it was then time to select individuals to be questioned to be a part of the jury. Imagine a 'bingo-like' machine that they used to randomly select cards that had our names on them. A hand reached in to grab the first one. My inner voice "Don't be me, don't be me… It's not going to be me…" (a longer pause introspectively) "Oh wait, it's going to be me."

They call out "Melanie" Juror number 1. (Me!)

What are the odds?! Granted it was a one-in-45 shot, but still.

We were instructed by the judge to be fair jurors, judge the credibility of the witness equally regardless of their position in law enforcement or not, and that the defendant is innocent till proven guilty, among other points.

All in all, the trial lasted a week and we listened to four witnesses — and it was an emotional ride. The jury was made up of 12 people and we had three alternates. A diverse group of people in age, ethnicity, gender identity, height, and those diversities unseen and not perceived by the human eye.

Although we entered the room as strangers from different walks of life, we were all there united under a common cause for justice.

When it came to deliberations, as juror number one, I was the foreperson. Essentially I learned from the judge that I would be the person to ensure that everyone's voice was heard, be the one to request evidence, and then... deliver the verdict in the courtroom.

Oh gosh.

After analyzing all the evidence, we eventually came to a verdict which reflected what we saw, heard, and felt.

Guilty.

I signed the verdict sheet and then the court officer validated what I signed. I was then handed a white envelope with 'Verdict' in black ink. I never knew a piece of paper could feel so heavy.

Another juror asked me "How do you feel?"

And I replied, "The only way I can do this is by separating myself from my emotions."

My heart was racing. Pounding. Fast. The fate of someone was in my hands.

Walking into the courtroom all eyes on us. Everyone in anticipation of the news that only the 12 of us in the entire world knew, and me, the one responsible to share it. (Me!)

"Please rise."

When I stood, another woman, whom I had never seen before, started reading the first charge and then passed the ball to my court. My heartbeat was echoing across my entire body. I opened the envelope then the paper. Slowly and meticulously.

I looked up and said "We the jury… find the defendant guilty."

I could hear and feel the nerves in my own voice.

We were asked by both lawyers to repeat back if we all agreed with the verdict. A symphony of guilty. I got one last look at the defendant and my heart truly ached. I saw the humanity in the person and separated them from their crime.

And that was it. We were thanked for our service and waited till we got our lunch that we so deserved. I wanted my cheese calzone. (Love a cheese calzone!)

When I eventually got home, I popped. An emotional rainbow filled with many, many tears. Charged with sadness over systemic racism, lack of accessibility, access, and equity to name a few. Wondering why people make certain decisions and who they are impacted by to make those decisions. The empathic and sensitive person in me was emotionally exhausted— praying that the defendant finds light at the end of the tunnel and has hope for better days ahead. As a multi-racial person and family, this all hits hard. I was, and am, so grateful to have been comforted by my loved ones when I needed it.

Having come out of jury duty weeks ago, this experience taught me that you are put in situations that you may not be mentally prepared for, but there are bigger plans and powers at work. I believe that.

I kept questioning "Why me? Why was I assigned to this case and randomly selected to be the foreperson?" Perhaps it wasn't so random. I guess it was written in my stars. You know what, "Why not me?" I was so nervous and scared… yes… but I did it. I did it anyway. And now it is another layer to the person I am. Another experience that makes up the mosaic of me.

55

For me, this jury duty experience was a culmination of all that I was challenging myself within 2023: strengthening how to trust my instincts, nurturing myself out of my comfort zone, and embracing the rainbow of valid emotions.

Progressing in growth and wisdom,

Melanie A. Greene

By Darlene Cervantes
Username: darleenc5

Witness To Our Love

I look back to that photo,
The one that's framed above my desk.

It's not because we ventured out,
Or because we loved the art.

Could it be the night-lit sky,
Musicians, the star-lit vibe?
Or perhaps it was blatantly
our anniversary.

Looking back I know
it was just that moment.
The passerby, the photographer

became a witness to that instant.
Capturing the moment, the glimmer in our eyes.

Arms around my hips
Eyes locked into mine.
Smile awakening dimples
Lashes rising to the sky.
Hearts beating peacefully
yet excitedly.
Yearning to be confined in this moment,
My favorite moment of 2023.

Avoiding my departure,
Detached from visa concerns.
Come to think of it,
The origin of our flags.
Both holding stripes,
same direction, towards the horizon.
Different colors,
apparently a huge difference.
They want red and white.
While his, nature green and sunny yellow.
Stars, same placement
But his, missing only 49.
I think about that every day
Painfully waiting for the approval.
But I didn't dare to think that night.
It would've tarnished that moment.

A perfect moment,
One where we are together.
Better together, just like the song.

Not thinking about our **LDR** (long distance relationship).
Only two strangers that had just met the year before.
Look at us now.

Two souls forever in love,
Carrying that moment,
Our favorite moment.

Darlene Cervantes

By Morgan Bland
Username: dlamdiva

Just One Good Day

Endless days bleed together
Troubles run one into the next
Drowning in a flood of bills
Home a rundown prison I can't fix
Watching, waiting for December
To slow the hardships steady parade
Biding time to take my flight
And seize just one good day

Tossed and battered by life's unyielding storm
Guided only by my siren's soothing song
Twelve months fighting a constant battle
Brought me back where I belong
If I had to starve, beg, borrow, steal,

Or sell all I own, it'd be worth the trade
For this moment, shinier than diamond,
Worth more than gold, just one good day
Dying fires of hope rekindle, burning bright
As the lights against a New York skyline
Evergreen eyes outshine the decorated trees,
Seeing past my flaws as they gaze into mine
Those kind eyes and encouraging words
Sustain me until I can find my way
Back to this place in a different time
Reunited for just one good day

Morgan Bland

By Danéa Summerford
Username: lancaielysian

_____

Epiphany

There are about 8,760 hours in a year, which we break down into 24 per 365 days. There's a lot of time within a single year, and even as I'm writing this on December 21, there are still so many hours in which things can happen. Looking back at the year from the start to now, so many things could have happened, and many things should have happened.

Six months ago, if you asked me what my favorite moment of the year had been, I'd probably have told you something about a boy, a particular boy for whom I've kept my feelings hidden for a long time. Naturally, I've feared rejection for many years of my life due to unhealed trauma. I spent so many moments with this particular six-foot-something, brown-eyed boy, not all of which were "good" that I could choose from. Perhaps six months ago, I would have told you it was the day I first laid eyes on him, and though I didn't realize it at the time, my soul had recognized him. The attraction was strong enough that I'd be drawn to him like a magnet no matter how far apart we were. I may have said that it was the first time we ever touched intimately, and I discovered things about me that I did not consciously know existed.

I can tell you that six months ago, and even now, I would not have said my favorite moments were the ones in which the "friends" I thought I had betrayed me. I would not choose the moment when the boy I cared for so much and was willing to do so much for had played directly in my face and then justified his actions with, "You're not my girlfriend." However, all of the "bad" things, the fake friends, the people who only stayed in my life because I had something to offer them but didn't care about me at all, the boys who touched me without my consent, the ones that used me, that discarded me the second that I was no longer providing what they wanted, the people who would have left me out in the cold without second thought if it meant they'd be warm, were all essential people in my life who played major roles. I will tell you that I have forgiven every single one of them. Not because I believe they deserve it, though I do, or because I miss them, but because I learned that I deserve that same forgiveness from myself for allowing them to do what they've done. I can also tell you that it was tough to come to this conclusion, but I did it anyway.

After I'd lost nearly everything: friends, family, material possessions, money, and time, I found that I had something even better. Love. Amid the chaos that 2023 had been, I always had a pure, kind, and loving soul. I had cried and questioned the Universe, asking why I had to go through what I did and why those things were happening to me, and for a good while, I hadn't received an answer. I was close to giving up hope, close to becoming the people who'd hurt me, but I persevered. I wept, prayed, ran from my shadows, and then made the conscious choice to face them, to choose peace instead of chaos, stay true to myself and my heart, choose not to take revenge, and choose to be better. And on December 19, at around 4:25 am, I decided to start listening. Not to what other humans would say, not to logic, not to the voice in my head that told me to hate and fear, but to the Universe. I fell into a meditative state, which, up until that point, had always been a little tricky for me. Of course, my mind first traveled to that boy, who'd, for the life of me, never left my mind for long since the day we met. My mind, or perhaps it was my angels, my guides, took me to a place where I talked to his mother, and she asked me, "What is it you see in him?" And the first answer came so easily, "his light." It's what attracted me after all, but that wasn't quite deep enough; there was so much more to it, and so I tried a few more times. His soul, his spirit again—it was certainly not anything he had done for me when he'd done nothing at all. Though very attractive, his looks had nothing to do with it. Eventually, I told her, "I see myself." This realization threw me into a rabbit hole of memories with and without him. I recalled every upset and jealous moment I had of him, and I realized that my problems had never truly been with him; I'd forgiven him every single time, but they were with me. I just refused to see those hidden shadow aspects that weren't so hidden but were ignored.

At that point, the questions to my prayers had been answered. "Why me?" because I was strong enough to face it; I was strong enough to endure. "Why did they do that to me?" because had they done it to anyone else, they would've been met with fear or hate over the kindness and love I'd shown them. I needed to learn to forgive myself, and the Universe used them for that lesson. It was me because my heart and soul are made of pure, forgiving love. I then understood that it was much bigger than myself; I could see how I was pure light for those people, whether they realized it or not, that I was their blessing and their lesson, and they were mine. So, my favorite moment of this past year was when I realized my purpose on December 19, around 6:22 am.

Danéa Summerford

By Tasha Uliano
Username: tashafierce

To My Shelter Dog

I walked into the shelter looking for a friend. I wanted a
small dog because I thought I would be one of those girls
to carry my dog around in my purse everywhere. I walked
around and all the dogs were barking and running around
their little enclosures. I stumbled upon you. They called you
Oreo because you were black and white. You were curled
up in a little ball, not barking, not excited. I thought, "She's
small." I asked to see you more than through the bars of
your enclosure. You stood up as I approached you and I
noticed you were a little bigger than I thought. I didn't
mind, you were a gem. Coincidentally, you had a white
diamond centered in the middle of the black fur on the back
of your neck. We played and you seemed so happy now that
you weren't trapped in there. My little pit bull, so sweet,

so sad and so sick. I decided I would take you home. For weeks you were on medication. You were coughing, so much snot was coming out of your nose. I diligently took you to your doctor's appointments. I was worried and I hoped you would make it through this. Eventually, you did. You became so strong and muscular. I wondered how since we went on the same walks, and my legs didn't look like that. You were now 50 pounds, a long way from the dog that came in as a stray.

People say, "It's so nice that you rescued a dog." No one ever said how nice it was of her to rescue me. I didn't keep the name Oreo, you were a Marla Ann. You're a diva. You sleep with more pillows than people do. You give people the side eye that are acting up. Bikes and skateboards make you feel on edge. You smile when you're excited. You are always so happy to see me. You always want to cuddle with me. You comfort me when I am sad, when I am cold, and when I am happy. You taught me how to be selfless—how to care about something other than myself. I was starting to slip before I found you. You keep me company when I'm lonely, you motivate me when I feel lazy. I may have given you a house to live in, but you made my house a home. I am so grateful for you, thanks for rescuing me.

A Dog Mom

By Anastasia Quintanilla
Username: sashamaq24

Lifesaver

I can't describe how it felt when we met for the first time
It was like he brought color to my life
All by himself
And the trees started singing
The wind was screaming
The earth stopped
I remember how nervous you were
He asked me to see his fridge
And for the first time in my life
I laughed so hard, I had forgotten how good it was to laugh
Meeting him became my favorite core memory

Anastasia

By Hannah Gonneville
Usename: hangon

---

68 **Birthday Bliss**

I have to say that 2023 has been pretty kind to me. It's been a good year and I've embarked on adventures that I never would've imagined in my wildest dreams. That being said, it was difficult to choose my favorite moment of the year, however one rises above all the others.

Picture this…

It was my birthday. The July heat warmed my face as I woke to the sound of kids playing at a nearby park in the suburbs of Chicago. I was a long way from my home in Maine, but it didn't feel that way because my other half—my better half—my twin sister was sleeping in the room next door. I woke with gratitude for another day, for a new year of life beginning, for the life of my sister (who is my best friend), for the chance to do life together, and much more. I say a quick prayer thanking God for these blessings as I soak up the rays of sun shining through the window and wait for my sleepy sister to wake up.

Our first adventure of the day was to get to Starbucks to get our free birthday beverage. As she sipped on her iced caramel macchiato and I sipped on my honey flat white, we walked to a nearby nail salon to get pedicures, all the while chatting about our hopes, dreams, and goals for the next year.

When we reached the nail salon, we settled in for some rest and relaxation. I chose a lighter purple color and my sister chose a pale blue color. The shades of nail polish we chose are total opposites, yet complement each other quite well, just like my sister and I do. I looked over to her as she was getting her nails done and saw her smiling and I smiled, too, knowing that she was happy.

With our tummies rumbling we headed over to P-Quads, a deep-dish pizza restaurant that both my sister and my dad raved about. As we walked in, the heavenly smell of pizza cooking wafted its way to my nose. We ordered a pepperoni deep-dish pizza and devoured several slices of pizza before tapping out.

We headed back to my sister's apartment and got ready for the main reason I was in Chicago (besides seeing my sister) to see Ed Sheeran perform in Soldier Field. The previous Christmas, my sister had gotten me tickets to the concert. I had waited for this for half a year and now it was here. The anticipation and excitement grew as I got ready.

Before leaving for the concert, my sister and I blew out our candles and had a few bites of our cheesecakes that we had ordered from the Cheesecake Factory a few days before. Each bite was creamy, delicious, and super rich.

Finally, we left for the concert. We arrived at Soldier Field and walked up to the humongous stadium. Khalid came out and the excitement was palpable. With enthusiasm and energy, he worked the whole crowd. With the excitement at its peak, Ed Sheeran came bounding onstage. I could not believe I was actually there. I have been a fan of his for a long time and here he was in the same vicinity as me. You could say I was a little star-struck, even though Ed is such a humble guy. More than that, a feeling of deep wonder and gratitude filled my being. How this birthday was so different from the last birthday I had where I'd spent the day alone, grieving the loss of my grandparents, wondering if I was seen or known. Ed sang his little heart out and the crowd shared moments of joy, laughter, and tears as we sang along to his songs. As the concert was about to end, Ed instructed us to take out our phone and use our flashlight on our phone. As he sang, we waved our phones in the air as we took in the lyrics, the melody, and the moment.

I have to admit that 2023 has been kind to me and that there have been many good moments this year, but this one tops them all. It was a perfect day spent with one of my favorite people, treating ourselves, eating good food, and watching one of my favorite pop artists send lyrics that encapsulate both the beauty and messiness of life into the humid night air. I felt at peace. I felt seen and known in the moment. I could not help but smile from ear to ear and soak in each moment. And even now the memory washes over me and fills me with a wonder and gratitude that I know I will remember for the rest of my life.

Hannah G.

By Sole Love
Username: 80hdsole

_____

Exist

It was a perfect day. Full of bliss and uninterrupted catalysts.
No walls and no towers, just ancient trees and clustered flowers.
The sun was our only light, and soon come the moon to announce the night.
But on this day, in this space, we can bathe in the rays.
We can exist until the day chooses to desist, we can lay in the place Mother Nature has kissed.
We can indulge in the beauty or divulge our perspicuity.
Show one another how we view the thoughts of Carruthers and the colors that always manage to decorate our summers.

Tree and breathe, gentle breeze, I relish in the wake of your expertise.
The warmth of your essence filled the space with ease.
And there we chose to be, as that is where we may find peace nestled beneath our feet.
Not runners, no flutter, but a violent thunder causes the world to shutter. We've found one another.
We resolve disunity with skulls of ambiguity and intellectual acuity.
We release and resist, an id-driven egotist and her catechist, lost in the air of mindlessness and minds less missed.
On this day, in this space, we simply bathe in the rays.
We were the only light and soon came the moon to announce the night.
No walls, no towers, just burning trees and special flowers.
It was a perfect day. Full of bliss and uninterrupted catalysts.

Sole Love

By Alexis McWhorter
Username: alexisjanine

My Journal: November 11th, 2023

Dear Me,

Today has been one for the books (Easily the best day of this year)!

There were so many factors that made this day extraordinary! What is most important, though, is the fact I was able to unveil three new discoveries all in one day!

For starters, I stepped outside of my comfort zone. Being in Asheville, especially on a Saturday, I normally go to the same places and restaurants downtown, but not this time. I tried a variety of different foods and drinks. For the food portion, my personal favorite had to be the Nashville Hot

Tofu. For the drink, the one that stood out to me most was called the Green Monster. Not the energy drink, rather, a Boston alcoholic drink. (Since those discoveries, I have now gone pescatarian knowing there are still so many amazing and tasty options while being on a well-balanced diet.)

Further, the entirety of the vacation was a mother-daughter bonding experience. When you bond with someone that means so much to you, you are able to really take a genuine interest and learn even more about each other. For the first time, Mama said she viewed me as one of her best friends! Hearing that alone comforts my heart knowing I have finally achieved the relationship I have also longed for with her.

Last, but certainly not least … you found yourself, Alexis! You found who you truly want to be in life.

…I don't want to be just one thing.
I want to be EVERYTHING I can be.

Love ♥,
Yourself

Alexis McWhorter

By Aimee Concepcion
Username: aimeevc

Green

Most people, when they think of green, they think of trees, grass, simple things. When I think of green, I think of my whole life. My future wife. It's hard to think of you in such simple ways, you're vast. Even with your past, you still find ways to laugh and smile. I'd drag my bloody feet a thousand miles just to see you smile. I still can't believe it. I used to think of green in simple ways but now I've parted ways. Because the thought of you is so deeply intertwined in my mind it makes me go blind. I can't see anything but you and that'll forever be true. I'll hold my breath until my face turns blue and pass out until I can once again be with you. You are not simple, you are vast. Like the forest that forever lasts. You give me air in my lungs and I can finally breathe again. Maybe you are like a tree. Something so simple yet so vital to my being. I look into your eyes and I just can't unbind. I want to get lost in your world, I can't believe the universe gave me this girl. I used to not like the color green, but now I search for it in everything I do because the color green always reminds me of you.

Aimeevc

By Grace Catan
Username: gracecatan

———————————

The Night We Turned The Porch Light On

there is always more
of you to love

this month i learned to throw a punch
with painted nails from girls who loved
to yell and sing covered in blood
and huff and cry to feel enough
of who we are beneath these gloves
we sang Let It
Go
to card games and birthday cakes
to your forks and my plates
with Green Light in the background
the porch's bulb, the dancing

sound, the alarm to cower
if you burn a witch

can i have this dance
called theater, kids
too tipsy to know the rules
when the cards are dealt
on coffee spills
and yet cackles abound

hidden crunch bars in pockets
whipped cream on faces
drama we missed
drawn out banter
all a new good place
yogurt, flavor of the year
only marks the clock's ticks
i was never ready to get
on that plane when I lent you my polo
i spun in that chair like a 'coaster
to stop the spilling of spirits
to guard this tender ticker

this place showed me
how to find more to love in

waffles and berries and potato soup
and essays that taught us to punch

holes in bags of delicate lies
reveal a world of shared desires
in the sunshine that rays from our lips
and the leisure with which we exist
together
expanding with
each forehead kiss, my third
carry-on premonitions
until our next collision

Grace Catan

By Ray Whitaker
Username: whitjr

———————————

Black Moose

It resonates with me
my encounter with another mysticism of nature
at the edge of the mountain glen.
While chancing to be near it
the large, black mass standing stationary in the aspens
as if to be unnoticed by being still

a bull moose eating leaves from above it's head
a thin line of silver fur
going from mighty shoulder to mid back
young antlers soon to be a fierce armament
now in velvet, growing
as if to scoop up the world.

Moving closer
keeping a mature pine betwixt
the likely over a thousand pounds of magnificence
and my wonder

thus occupied I did not worry
when he stopped eating
looking in my direction
standing there wondering about me perhaps
as he stood in the dappled sunlight.
Astonished at the proximity
noticing the depth of these brown eyes
pushing souls together, mine to his
brown, mine, to brown, his
iris' different, mine round, his oval

being in the moment of no thought
now wondering if he had a name
no feeling of fear in that closeness
only around twenty paces separating us
the sun shone on me as I looked
and as if I felt that regal power-black fur
a strength, assurance, commanding the ground
he stood on, like owning the very earth.

He is next to my tree now
having moved so silently
and keeping the thick pine between us,

our eyes locked still
getting what each other had to give
my consciousness mingling
with the being of this immense creature
his long neck craning around, reaching nearly in my space.

I moved away, breaking the mesh
keeping the pine tree between we two
having realized this tree
was woefully small
having become a wood beetle now uncovered under the bark
I retreated to the next few tall pines nearby.

I am the Rhinoceros Beetle now.

Our conversation had not ended
though no words had been spoken out loud
no malice felt, only a near wistfulness
from the moose and I.

Like a translator would be appreciated
to move the instances together somehow

staring into each other's eyes
for longer still
feeling the thoughts
each having our own insights

of consciousness
and intuitiveness

that powerful rippling muscled black now moving away
my humanness moved in this moment.

Even wanting to know where all this would go
I did not follow deeper into this thicket, his woods.

Ray Whitaker

By Sarah Perez
Usename: sarita

Perfect Doesn't Sum It Up

Sunlight drips through the ancient trees

It drips into my skin
Warming me in the cool forest.
The warmth of the Universe tells me I am Home

I am at home in Nature surrounded by laughter of girls
becoming the young woman that will change the world

I see their Magic
I see their Power
I see their Weirdness

And I remember the Joy of being that Girl
Weird
Smart
Ambitious
The world ahead of me Vast and Limitless
And my only wish for all the
Weird
Smart
Ambitious
Girls of the World is that they have the Courage,
Confidence, and Character
to make this life and Earth better for all of us

After searching my whole life for that feeling of
Peace and Promise
I found it

Drenched in sunlight, laughter, and song
Smelling of dust and dew
Just to be me in this place is more than I could have ever
dreamed

Sarah

By Rashan Speller
Username: artistphilly

———————————

Thank You From
A Phone Call

It's supreme to see the difference between guided
meditations between poets. The way one's words can give
spirit the will to steer a movement. And the lost of the
spoken word to perform in front of Gods when it's lost in
moments. This pine box that kept locked? The pillars of
actions, and thoughts which keep me in motion. It's these
times when a call from God can give you the courage to
defeat the cowardice of self-service to society's involvements.
But it came from an unsealed person, who wasn't washed by
the addictions of personal cues to batter the isolated person.
A personified hue-man who gave me the impression of being

a super soldier. So buried alive was the feeling that my words weren't enough to spread a revolution.

Rashan Speller

By Emily Warner
Username: ewarner

To You My Dearest Stranger

To Whomever Finds Themselves Reading This Letter,

To you, my dearest stranger, you'd never believe yourself if
end of the year you told beginning of the year you all that
the year would bring, all the good and bad and everything
in between. Yet, if I had the opportunity to talk to January
me, I'd tell myself that I was going to be forced out of my
comfort zone, embraced by new friends, and plunged into
a sea of unknowns. It'd all be worth it though, since I'd be
coming out the other side a better version of myself.

With 365 chances to experience life, unfortunately,
it sometimes feels as though the days slip by or blur
together, but this year there was one day in particular

that undoubtedly was the best and became my favorite — September 3rd. After this day, my life felt like it spun around on its axis and that I finally came up to take that long-awaited breath of fresh air.

Like many great things in life, September 3rd was unexpected. It initially started as the day I'd finally meet up with a random online group I had joined over a year before. I saw it as a fun opportunity to meet new people and worst-case scenario, I never had to see them again if it didn't go well. Carpe diem, right?

Ironically, soon after saying 'yes' to attending this hangout, I was also convinced to go skydiving the morning before our big meetup. Not only would I finally be marking off one of the top items that had been dangling on my bucket list for as long as I could recall, but I'd also be doing so with a bunch of strangers.

September 3rd awakened with sunny rays, blue skies, and on-edge nerves. Even as I drove up to the airstrip, even as I signed a 12-page waiver, and even still as I stepped into my harness, I couldn't believe today was the day I could actually accomplish such a monumental thing. Surrounded by strangers, embraced with contagiously bright energy, we soared to 13,000 feet, jumped into the clouds, and felt blissfully free. A spike of fear, rush of adrenaline, and pure, ecstatic joy all filled my core. Freefalling was incomparable to anything else I had ever experienced and it was everything I wanted it to be. When the last of us stepped foot back on solid ground, an unspoken pact of friendship was already formed, even if we didn't know it yet.

After a morning like that, what better way to continue the day than to attend the actual hangout that began it all. Meeting up with my skydive buddies again, we gathered on the beach and soon more and more people arrived. We listened to music, ate, drank, swam, and talked the day away. No matter which way I turned, no matter which stranger I talked to, I was met with smiles, laughter, and genuine conversation.

Our festivities continued until the sun set and darkness covered the beach, except no one was ready to say goodbye. Hopping over to the nearby bars, we began dancing. And danced we did, until we couldn't anymore. Hopping, spinning, twirling, head banging, and moving any way the music took us, happiness surrounded us all.

Barely believing the clock, we wrapped up our day 21 hours after it all began. As I rested my head back on my pillow that night, I could hardly believe all that happened that day, how much I truly felt fully alive, and how genuine the people were. It's something special when strangers can come together and instantly have an authentic connection about life, passions, and the dreams we share. Though I hoped to see these kind-hearted, incredible individuals again one day, September 3rd me would never believe what was soon to come my way. How so many of the 'strangers' I met that day would very soon become intertwined into my life and me into theirs.

Call it destiny, irony, coincidence, chance, or just life; our stories now all include each other. The days, weeks, and months following September 3rd were packed, near overflowing, with new life experiences. I now found myself surrounded by profound opportunities to make memories with these strangers who unexpectedly and effortlessly became some of my nearest and dearest friends.

So to you, my other fellow, dear stranger, think twice next time you are given the opportunity to say yes to an experience, to start a conversation with someone new, or the chance to step outside of your comfort zone. The unknown, that's right on the other side of something you may fear, might just be exactly what your life and soul needs.

Yours truly,

Emily

By Karen Rice
Username: kmimsrice

_____

Hearing The Sound
Of Those Words

I've had many memorable days and moments within 2023 that I will never forget. All involve my daughter and grandkids. These were days I thought a couple times during my life I would never see, due to two cancer diagnoses. So, those days will always be the best days of my life. There's no other days better. But I must say, one day in particular I will never forget, and I received it so gracefully. That day would be November 10, 2023. It would be the day I received the words, "No Cancer Found." Yes, just at the time of year I was diagnosed previously, right around the holidays. I had a couple symptoms that made my MD, as well as myself, think the big "C" may have returned. On this very special precious day, I was told all was good and all tests came back negative. That's all I wanted to hear during the holidays. It was one of the greatest gifts to myself, after my children. I had been feeling down thinking it would ruin my holidays yet again, but God!

Karen Rice

By Maggie Faye
Username: maggiefaye

———————————

The Best Day

The best day is a slow day at work. The best day is the day that the sun is shining, but it's not too hot outside. The best day is the first day the temperature drops in September. The best day is the day I can give my baby a kiss. The best day is the day I belly laugh with my best friends until my cheeks hurt. The best day is the day I give my mom a hug. The best day is the day I am loving and kind on purpose. The best day is the day without anxiety; the day I can breathe through it. The best day is the day I start a new book. The best day is the day I finish my new favorite book. The best day is the day I start knitting, and every day I get to since. The best day is the day I get to go on adventures with the people I love. The best day is going to the Atlanta Zoo with my oldest sister and our partners. The best day is that same day, at the zoo, when a lion made eye contact with me (I swear it's true). The best day is in Boston, watching the second oldest sister graduate from Harvard. The best day is reconnecting with extended family for the first time in a decade in Boston. The best day is the day I went to the Hozier concert, and I was physically connected to the music and the message more than ever before. Everyone in the audience was crying and it was beautiful. The best day is the day I realized my chronic illness is teaching me how to stop and rest. The best day is the day my cat decides he wants to snuggle in my lap before bed. The best day is therapy day! The best day is the day I realized I am healing; my hard work is paying off. The best day is the day I let myself cry in front of someone else. The best day is the day I realize I'm as smart as I think I am and, yes, I can prove it to you. The best day is the day I decide to be brave. The best day is the day I do the brave thing.

Maggie Faye

By Nicole Hughes
Username: eveandthesnake

_____

A Silver Lining

The day: Sun shining; Vibrancy surrounds.

Within me, a deep gloom, blocking the sun. Torturous
thoughts, my demons, gnawing at my sanity and casting
flesh to past buried bones and taunting me with the sad
memories of my distant childhood. This occurrence was not
unusual in my life, and every time it happened I'd be furious
with myself for allowing it to have so much power over me.
"Why can't I just let it go? It's not happening anymore"
is what I'd say to myself. But something was different this
time. I felt a call to dive into this darkness—not to run
away from the uncomfortable emotions, but to be present for
them. So, I invited the demon in. I sat with her. I listened
as she told me her story, and why she was in so much

pain and of the abuses she endured. The more I listened with compassion and love, the more she'd transform. I wiped her tears and caressed her hair. I told her that it wasn't her fault — that she was safe now. I felt her rumblings calm into the warmth of the day, the light revealing to me what was not a demon at all, but a scared little girl in need of care and protection. And, from then on, that's what I gave her.

Nicole Hughes

By Famo Musa
Username: famomusa

_____

The Day Of My Dreams

In the early hours of May morning
a symphony of life, a world reborn
the air tastes crisp, with a touch of dew
as nature awakens, I feel a jolt at the base of my spine
This was different from the others I felt.

My doctor told me to walk you out
the time was near, so I heed her advice
the sun's kiss warms the earth's embrace
as flowers bloom in a vibrant race
the birds singing in a joyous delight
their melodies dance in the morning light
and I feel your flutters as I jog throughout
both in anticipation of our first meeting

a gentle breeze whispers secrets untold
as leaves flourish in the zephyr's hold
the world is a canvas, fresh and bright
in the clutch of a spring morning's light
a day to feel the breath of air's kiss
surrounded by forest green grass
I imagine your first cry as an angel's melody.

the fragrance of earth blows sweet air into the atmosphere
and fills the senses with scents so complete
spring is like a hope that is going to take a renewal flight
as I await your arrival to Earth.

So in the stillness of the new day
a May's evening's beauty lights the way
It's a promise of life, a feeling so bright
a gift from nature, in the moon's glow
my favorite kind of day ended with you
in my arms as they placed you on my chest
May 15th will forever be my favorite kind of day
the day you light up my spirit with your presence.

Famo Musa

By Rayven Washington
Username: rayven_butanyways_prettylady

_____

You, ME, & 2023

Traveling this skyline for you
Taking flights throughout the night for you
When I met you
You turn all my fears to reals
Turing my possibilities to my reality truth
One day, looking forward to standing right in front of you
Holding your hands
And saying I DO
We will be decked out
In our favorite new suits
Nevertheless my best
Was when I met you on June 20th, 2023
It was our greatest test
We hardly slept and got any rest

Sleepless nights
This love feels so calendar nice
Never second-guessing
At first, our trust issues got the best
But that wasn't the end nor the rest
Falling in love with who I am
Falling in love with this woman
Cause now all I can say is **I CAN**

Rayven Washington

By Julia McCarty
Username: jmccarty

Graduation Day

How did I get here?
Yesterday was my first day of school
I think I blinked and now I'm done
It's really almost cruel

My eyes were open before the sun
could wink its first few rays
Went through my usual morning routine
It was just another day

But suddenly my shoes didn't fit
My dress was way too tight
My gown looked wrinkled and needed an iron
Makeup wouldn't sit quite right

"Today of all days!" I thought in dismay
I tried to take a deep breath
I started to sweat, started to fret
Oh, but it wasn't over yet

"I know I signed up months ago!"
Now I was starting to panic
"I'm sorry," she said, "You're not on the list!"
I think I'm going to be sick

Truth be told, I was dreading this day
Long before it came
It meant the end of what I knew
Where everything was the same

I'm standing on the precipice of change
The long and winding road that is the rest of my life
Looming large and unfamiliar
Past and future balanced on the point of a knife

It's all worked out, I step in line
Pomp and Circumstance ringing in my ears
No time to look, no time to run
Time to face the music, face the fears

The lights are blinding, I squint and stare
I look up and I finally see

All the people in the world I love
Come all this way for me

The show is a blur I can barely remember
Laughing and crying all the while
With careful steps I cross the stage
Accept my diploma with a smile

It's not so bad on the other side
I cautiously consider
What was I so afraid of?
(Besides getting old and bitter)

"You'll be chasing that high forever,
All downhill from here," they say
Your life doesn't end after school
It starts on Graduation Day

Julia McCarty

By Oswald Perez
Username: opwriter

A Long Day's Journey Into The Night In Iraklio

Dear Unsealers:

2023 is rapidly coming to a close.
365 days have come and gone.
Yet, one particular day this year stands out from the rest.

It was Sunday, October 1st.

After spending a week running around mainland Greece,
our group boarded a plane departing from Athens and
arrived on the island of Crete. Kalimera to the city of
Heraklion.

By Oswald Perez
Username: opwriter

Island time had kicked in with a later start. But it would be a busy day nonetheless.

Our first stop brought us to the archeological site at Knossos. The open air seat of the Minoan civilization. The labyrinth was underneath our feet, alas, there was no sign of the mythic Minotaur around.

The next stop was to the Titakis Winery.

A tour of the vineyard began amongst the vines — walking through vines and picking off the grapes to eat. The production process was explained further before we tasted the wine. Two tables under blue skies, sunshine, and four different wines. Each one getting its due.

Further around the island, we went for lunch. It would be a multi-course affair with abundant food and conversation. At this point of the trip, our group had become like family. For good measure, the meal finished with a round of the liquor Ouzo. Don't be fooled by its clarity, the drink packs quite a punch.

As we arrived back at the hotel, the day wasn't over yet.

Upon arriving at the hotel the day before, I had seen the logo of the soccer club AEK Athens in the conference room nearby. I didn't understand the reason why it was there, though.

As I made my way up to the hotel's lobby, the sound of soccer chants filled the air. There was a big smile on my face, the star-struck look on our guide's face, as AEK is the soccer team her and her sons support, and bewilderment from everyone else. AEK Athens was in town for a match against the local side OFI Crete F.C.

The group of thirty-two became thirty-six as a pair of college students and a pair of professional Greek dancers joined us on the bus heading to dinner. The sun set over Iraklio as day turned to night.

We arrived at a taverna on the other side of the island. Nary a soul around as we walked up the steps to the terrace. Tables laid out below the vine covered roof. And on the horizon, a full moon changing colors in the sky.

The meal began with a pair of musicians providing the soundtrack for the night. Without saying a word, the island's passion was felt.

After the meal was done and the dancers had shown us their moves, it was time for us to join the celebration and dance. The joy in the room was so strong, the ouzo that had been brought out wasn't needed.

I went up to the musicians to thank them for the music. I mentioned to them that I was a writer and a poet.

And one of them made a wish for me: that I would return to
Crete to spend the summer writing.

As I looked up at the full moon on the way back to the bus,
I knew it was an amazing day.

And there was still the visit to Santorini on the near horizon.

109

Oswald Perez

GOALS FOR THE
NEW YEAR

By Giselle Moran
Username: giselle

My Foes Are Your Foes

My foes are your foes
The troublesome foe —
everything you can become.
The future is anticipated,
but it has yet begun
the past is important
learn from it and grow
focus on yourself
and everything will follow
opportunity will arrive
when you least expect it
Pick up where you left off
Even when you forfeit
It can't be expedited —

it's written in the cards.
All you have to do,
is be who you truly are.

Giselle

By Julianna Waldvogel
Username: jewels

_____

The Next Legacy

New Year's Resolutions—
One I accomplished no slack,
Each check off the box,
Each proud moment to look back.

But in the last few years,
I've been slipping and failing.
Because of the busyness of life
That can be both great and heartbreaking.

Goals for this twenty twenty-four
Like anyone else has;
Weight loss, exercise, being healthy more,
Read books, invest in friendships,

Devotions, meditation, and journaling
For each morn to pass.

Don't forget being on a forgiveness journey
— To let go of offenses, be set free
From those long ago who did me dirty
And make me a better person, who I ought to be.

Will add more as I have dreams
Of writing stories for the whole world to see.
One book idea of a decade,
A screenplay, two, or more with
Fantastic scenes.

Yes, I love stories
— especially with themes
Happy, sad, funny, cry,
All to relate when life intervenes.

Now, the last resolution is only small,
"Life Dad up" is what's written on the list;
As pieces of my world fall
Bit by bit through illness's mist

It was one thing, then another,
Test given, test about
All came what was fully discovered:
Dementia. Was without a doctor's doubt.

Just like any year we're in
It's born, then dies,
Was his disease that stayed with
No intentions for goodbyes.

My Dad, my once strong hero,
My fright protector, and friend
In his place was someone different
In his dark corner—knowing he is coming close to a
complete end.

I have no fears for when he goes
to afterlife and farther.
But the one worry I do have is the day
he will no longer remember I am his daughter.

They say "You got your whole life ahead of you,"
Whenever I feel old
But "Life is short."
Is the truth to be told.

"Don't take the little things in life
for granted," another to say.
'Cause life is a gift, you never know
What comes in the day.

Knowing when it comes or unpredictable,
Emotions and thoughts come high and low

Tempted to give in despair
My Dad tells me his prayers for me to know:

"I want to leave behind a legacy of love,"
"Have faith, trust, and pray,"
"Work in what you love doing," and
"If you're led to do something, do it today."

Giving wisdom and advice for a lifetime
Like any parent would for their kid;
He's said many things but few I keep,
I realized my Dad's wisdom is never one to forbid.

So, I still follow my resolutions but with a hard,
yet good, approach for the year:
To keep writing, and to be present with family—
Both of which I hold to my heart so dear.

I must not give up—no, I mustn't!
My aim, my prayer, my wish, my goal:
Is to write, to publish, any story reaches the world
With heart and soul.

And for any story I write—
For any to be published, seen, and read;
For my Dad to witness, be proud, for a writing that treaded
In sweat and love to spread.

A gift, a talent, from father to daughter,
Each story inspired is never in vain.
A legacy placed before me with much encouragement,
support, and love —
A secret of life makes me the richest to gain.

118 *Julianna S Waldvogel*

By Dominique Nesbitt
Username: dommamomma

———————

Self-Love Letter
In Spoken Word

In 2024, I am believing in myself more —
feeling better than before,
with steady faith to stay the course.

Keeping commitments — despite conditions
— to what I truly care about;
keeping clarity of focus on the vision,
leaving no room for doubt.

I am stabilizing my foundation,
standing firm in what I know to be true.
I am focused on full self-adoration —
to see myself the way my loved ones do.

I am acknowledging and appreciating
all of my accomplishments,
as I paint the path—concentrating,
maintaining my confidence.

I can promise me, from this point on,
Whatever I do, I will do it purposely.
When I feel low, I'll sing self-love songs
with relief, and remember the worth in me…

because, in 2024, I am leaning toward
feeling better than before—
moving forever forward.

Dominique Nesbitt

By Jake April
Username: jsapril

_____

Air

Thinking about my goals for the new year makes me crouch
in my seat when I should sit up straight proud because
I got there

My brain **BURSTS**, mulling over **ANY AND EVERY
GOAL** so I take this time to look at them as a **WHOLE**

What do I have to do to complete this puzzle piece that is
comprised of **EVERY SINGLE GOAL?**

Being **CONFIDENT** and **PROUD** of what I have done
should give me all the reason to continue to strive for
SUCCESS this season

There is truly no reason why 2024 can NOT be a BREAKTHROUGH season

As I invision proceeding and SUCCEEDING in life, the reason I haven't had my breakthrough moment is easy

My potential is like the AIR you can NEVER have too much to spare

I don't dare to prepare to jump into the limitLESS air, BUT I am AFRAID of that STARE or smile that will inevitably be there (at least according to ME) to COMPARE

If I dare to run the race that is LIFE and I WIN, I will FOREVER WONDER if crossing that finish line FIRST was FAIR

I think about EVERYONE ELSE who CAN be there

Most certainly the guy with the limp is NOT supposed to be there (or so MYSELF thinks)

But I tell myself if I do NOT run the race (LIFE) like I BELONG, it will only be UNused air and WASTED air just means, in the end, I did NOT care and I MYSELF CARE

So, in 2024, I DARE to jump INTO MY limitLESS AIR!

Jake

By Alexis King
Username: aoking

Nothing

Was my resolution for this year,
at least the most public-facing
awkward, disheartening, and uninspiring
response, painfully clipped for the
question that I dreaded
and hoped to avoid?
Giving glitz to my hopefully mundane Monday
sitting in my dad's living room
for the only holiday we promised to him year after year
secretly too excited for the celebratory sips…
and every one in-between
Listening to his fiancée excitedly answer
this question for herself with pristine palatable promise
teaching her graduate classes staying true to herself

and making measurable progress
I... was desperately shying away from this year.
Cowering in the reality of all the
time that had passed. Running from the
truth that now another graduating class
could toast its glass
and the word "just" had to retire in a tired slink
before I scramble to explain the limbo
of "What's going on with me?"
Lagging, lacking, looking
I was supposed to, so supposedly set up for
so much, so many saw and swore I'd soar
like the bubbles in my drink
Now nothing.
While I dared not utter it
and draw attention to my unimpressive flailing
My true hope for this year, was for an end to the waiting
To begin my life and actual post-grad living and
wake up excited instead of no more than
Tolerant of how I'm living,
with kind of valid work connected
somewhat to what I enjoy doing
To be able to picture the future. Being able to see something
Sometimes it feels like it symbolizes no
longer existing
But this year I will walk away certified
learn the law of language and the art of icing
and placate the inner child

who sought peace these last few months
In the most mundane of things,
an opportunity to dress in costume,
a sip of boba tea, the chorus of a musical piece
My goal for this year is to see the other end
to thrive, reminisce on the strife, and how impatient
I was for a change in my life
chuckle lightly about my dramatic theatrics
And relish in the fact that after all,
I survived

Alexis King

125

By Autumn Harrington
Username: wintersummers1322

_____

The Simply Simples.

Another 1st of the year
Another round of
"resolution-ists' bullshit"

Another set … of another pair…
Of numbers.

No, no. No more numbers.
Just the year of
The More and The Less-es.
The Simples.
more kitchen ballet dances.
less quiet cries.
more lyrics that get ya'

less of the ones
that were used…
simply to manipulate
you.
more "look how far we've comes"
less "i'm supposed to be so much furthers"
More of the simply Simples.

More—
"i'm sorry I hurt you."
"i'm here if you wanna talk."
"we can get through this."
"how can I help?"
"it's gonna get better."
"thanks for having my back."
"i got you—always."
"you're stuck with me…"
"—promise?"
Always.

—xoxo A

Autumn Harrington

By Tracy Barnes
Username: poeticaddiction_365

My Reality Before I Turn 40

The expectations I set forth
Will allow me to light the torch
To a productive and successful 2024
Far beyond my imagination
This is the year of fulfillment
This is the year of new beginnings
This is the year that my consistency pays off
This is the year my dreams are my reality
My destiny awaits
I cherish the days of people saying
"I always knew you would"
"I always knew you were talented"
Not that I need the recognition
But I would be grateful that they were paying attention

I'm ready to enjoy the talent I was blessed with
Sharing it with the masses
I'm ready for my creativity to be heard
As well as read in the pages of my first poetry book
One of my biggest goals this year
Is to release a body of work
That represents me before I turn 40
This is the year
This is the year I dreamt of
This is the year that it all happens
Ain't nothing going to stop me but me
That's why this is the year of endless possibilities!

Tracy Barnes

By Raphael Inoa
Username: ralph_inoa

_____

130   # It All Starts This Year

This is it, Ralph
You've been gone for a while, but it's time to reappear
The pressure is all around you
Are you going to give in to the doubt?
Let the fear interfere?
Make excuses for yourself like you've done so for years,
As you sit back and watch your inner demons steer
Or are you finally going to take back the wheel,
Show the world, and make things clear
Of Ralph's resilience, who he really is, and why he's here
The choices you've made and the choices in sight,
Are the two factors in the equation that you call your life
What have you done,
And what will you do with this story you write?

What visions do you see? Any pinnacles you'll reach?
What mountains will you climb? What goals do you strive,
To accomplish in the physical as well as ones that are deep
inside?
A year from today, what achievements do you hope to
provide?

I'd have learned to break the shackles I'm confined,
To within the cage of my mind
To stop looking at the past and start paving a new path,
Of leaving an impact
To use my God-given talent, and not stand on the sidelines
To walk outside the lines,
Of my comfort where I often reside
I will find a way to better coexist,
With the inner demons that lie,
Within me
I'd have learned to break the shackles I'm confined,
To within the cage of my mind
To stop looking at the past and start paving a new path,
Of leaving an impact
To use my God-given talent, and not stand on the sidelines
To walk outside the lines,
Of my comfort where I often reside
I will find a way to better coexist,
With the inner demons that lie,
Within me
I will learn new things

Learn new places
Learn new limits, and exceed old ones
This year
I will keep my eyes set on the big dream
I will keep it alive
The blinding lights
The deafening rumble of the speakers all around the venue
Roaring out the words I've woven together
Looking out at hundreds,
Thousands,
Simultaneously doing the same
Simultaneously healing any pain,
We may have been going through
But for now
For this year,
I'll release the music that hundreds,
Thousands,
Will choose to overlook
With words that will roar out speakers,
of the most most humble venue
My room
Knowing all this,
I will still release the music
Solely,
Because I want to
Because I need to.
This year
I'll learn hope

I'll learn perseverance
I'll learn discipline
I'll learn growth
I'll learn patience
I'll learn success
I'll learn those,
And I'll learn me

I've seen your fight, and you've fought well
This next one is a little different
But I can tell,
You have what it takes
You must get out your shell
Do everything you said you will
Dust yourself off, get out that imaginary cell
Stick to your gut, and you will prevail
Make the tears worth it
Make the world see
Go ahead and put the work in,
And the people will soon enough believe

Thank you for having this talk with me
Or rather, with yourself
Afterall,
You are me, and I am you
The thing is, you know me
But I can't know you unless I live the rest of my life
The same exact way you have

You're right
But unfortunately,
I'm unable to give you more, and our time is up
Don't worry
You just proved to me you have everything you need
I hope that one day you can come back,
And view these words as me
If you can do that,
That's when you'll know

Know what?

You'll see
Farewell Ralph,
From here on out you'll need to turn it up a few gears
Everything you want:
It all,
Starts,
This,
Year.

Raphael Inoa

By Afton Villanueva
Username: poeticdiabetic

What Are Your Goals For Twenty Twenty-Four?

When hardships and trials are replacing everything you observe, understand; reality's giving ourselves a lesson. Some fail. Others realize that when excessive negativity's testing you, then we're experiencing nature teaching you faith — our ultimate reality.

My goals are to learn why I've been getting these life lessons and why life has blessed me with them. I want to start meditating daily, and para aprender más español. I want to see the opportunities offered to me as a port of unity that can help transform the views I see and want to see. I want to show gratitude for the small things in life and appreciate all that life has to offer. I want to become disciplined and have a healthy daily routine of eating and sleeping. I want to start revealing the new styles of writing I've been blessed to find while trying to realign my mind, such as this poetry collection of acronyms that I like to call Aftonyms. I also want to sell at least 100 of my books of poems called "Poetic Diabetic," and finish my second one called "Aftonyms."

Aw

By Tiara Smith
Username: tirasm

Beginning This Journey

My only major goal for this year: be my most authentic
self. I am embarking on a journey of self-discovery. To
accomplish this goal, I have set minor goals such as taking
sewing classes, going to the gym, learning aerial silks, and
so on. I've come to understand that experience is indeed the
best educator. Last year, I went ziplining for the first time.
Having a fear of heights, I was not expecting to enjoy it. I
let everyone go before me until I had no other choice. My
terror quickly turned into excitement as I went speeding
down the line. Sideways, upside down, spinning in circles,
and posing for pictures; I found another piece of my puzzle.
I realized how much life I had not lived. The last five
years of my twenties will be dedicated to unlocking parts

of myself. Letting myself be free. That is what I am most
excited about.

Tiara Smith

By Mel Taul
Username: itsedible

Fallow Year

My mind as the farmer, and my body as the land… This
year, we both get a break; It is my fallow year. I've spent
years planning, sewing, praying for rain, and harvesting
my crops; moving through life as if it were a check-off list to
turn in once completed. I, like soil, am depleted. I will meet
the weather patterns with ease, knowing I don't depend on
the rain. This year, I am a plot of land going untouched. I
am reclaiming rest, remembering — it is work. I am gifting
myself time to get back to my organic matter. I will accept
the pauses that come along with the fallow; unlike lost
income — my health cannot be replaced. I trust with time,
the earth will replenish my soil. I will welcome each sunrise,
simply grateful to see another day. I will accept droughts,

floods, pests, and the scorching summer heat. This year, I will move slowly, breaking the cycles one season at a time.

Mel Taul

By Hanna Gootée
Username: hgootee

——————

2024

Be here now. In the breath of the wind. In the rainbows of
the sunset. In the expressions walking across stranger's faces.

Be here fully. In the complexities of thought. In the vastness
of space. In the smells from the kitchen.

Be here lovingly. In the softness of forgiveness. In the
gentleness of joy. A hug, not a bow.

Time running out is such a gift; and this gift is a privilege to
be alive for.

Dark nights of the soul can be so convincing. Let this soften me.

Let this remind me-

Hope paints strokes of colors on the horizon
When the rest of the world is dark

All for us
Inexplicable beauty
The fade —
so subtle
While the deep red keeps hanging on
The higher we rise, the longer the colors last

An ode to keep chasing sunsets
To go through life with eyes wide open
Welcoming light and chasing great heights
For this day...
Is a reminder of hope
Even the darkest depths of the sky

Let me live life deeply.

Hanna Gootée

By Nicole Kisslinger
Username: nicoleskisslinger

Home Is Where I Go

To live a fulfilled life is to have one of value.
Lessons, tragedies, peaceful bliss, experiences.
I wish to make a home within myself; a home is where I'll go.

As the hours turn to days and days turn to months, I wish to
live a life worth living.

I wish to experience sunrises on the island, where blue
waves crash into the sand, being drawn by the current.
I wish to experience group circles filled with people from all
lands, telling stories of folklore and magic throughout the
full moon evenings.
I wish to experience long drives in a car, watching mountains

pass by my window as sunshine beams down on my face.
I wish to experience a feeling of deep peace in my soul and
create a home within myself, no matter where the wind
might take me.

As the hours turn to days and days turn to months, I wish to
feel alive.
I wish to feel at home.
For a home is where I go.

Nicole Kisslinger

By Liz Medina
Username: imlizkhalifa

Goals for 2024

I have so many goals for 2024.
This year will be bigger than before.

I will continue to mentor **ADHD** youth.
Advocate for **LGBTQ** to speak their truth.

January, Career Day inspiring young souls.
February, I'll accomplish one of my biggest goals.

In March, at a book gala with my own table.
April, youth art event, showing them of what they're able.

In May, we'll be on the cover of RallyUp Magazine.
June is Pride Month, what a beautiful scene.

July, we have a pop-up celebrating our success.
August, Unity Day for mental health awareness.

September, we're traveling to Mexico.
October, who knows where this path will go.

November, I'll be so grateful for the year that I had.
This year in December, the holidays won't feel so bad.

Liz Medina

By Astrida Hara
Username: astridahara

This Year, I Promise

This year, I promise myself
to not rely on someone to make the world better.
Rather, I will count on me,
to fill my role better on Earth.

This year,
I may not fulfill some hope in myself.
But I will do justice to my power.
I may not make much money.
But I will make more meaning.
I may have a lot of free time.
But I won't waste any minute.

For all the challenges,
the struggles,
the injustices,
the unwanted things that may happen to me this year,
I will face those bravely.

I will not fear any failure.
Because I can learn from them.
I will drink to my success,
Because I will deserve them.

I will not promise to be less sad.
But I promise I will be less mad.
I will not promise I will smile more.
But I promise I will be grateful more.

This year, I will write many books,
even though no one believes in me.
I will type and thrive,
cause I believe in myself.

Astrida Hara

By Chloe
Username: chloewritespoetry77

_____

"Arrival"

A poem for the new life I am bringing into the world in 2024.

I can't wait to meet you
Bright new life
clothed in vernix,
hair styled by nature,
sharing my every feature
as I learn to love them all
through you

When my body
can no longer hold you,
I will bring to life
the sun of early summer

drying all the rain
making everything green
and whole

I can't wait to know you
Eyes level with mine
Every goal realized
through you
My girl,
I've waited for so long
to be your mom

How long 'til I meet you?
I am bathed in sunlight
by the thought of your arrival
that will make us whole

CnSchultz

By Crystal Mulligan
Username: crystalmulligan

A New Day

The excitement you feel at new years. Is arbitrary. It's created. We decided that completing 365 days is an accomplishment. A time to celebrate, to reflect, to dream.

We begin to think about all the possibilities of a new year. The places we may go, people we may meet, people we may become.

We create the feeling of being new, fresh, opportunities await.

But what if we celebrated like this every week? Every day. We feel the same accomplishment and pride and joy for living another day. We feel the excitement and dream about the possibilities that tomorrow holds.

We truly, deep down, try to embrace the feelings of new years each and every day. We reflect on the day, what went wrong and release it. What went right and how we can foster more of that. Appreciate the places we went that day while dreaming of the places we'll go tomorrow.

We create how we feel. How we process. We can't control the outside influences, but we can work to control how we process and react. We can celebrate each and every day and the possibilities that a new day holds.

This year, I want to celebrate the new day.
Good morning, happy new day!
Good night, wishing you an amazing tomorrow!

Crystal Frances

By Jonathan Odle
Username: jlodle11

_____

2024: Crushing Goals And Walking In The Light

I'm fifteen days into the new year.
I've taken no more than twelve steps,
My eyes blink and in a flash I am here.
My 'empty' falls, I stand. In God's light, at my best.
An astral curtain, I've just phased through.
Sheer focus aimed ahead; no more playing dead.
Side not with the wicked; rather, the justly shrewd.
Most haven't seen what hell has to offer. I have, and I'm through.
I'll march forward. Alone, or with a few.
Nevermind those shadows, we walk in truth.
You've got me, and I've got you.

Jonathan Lee Odle

By Kelsea Guckin
Username: kelsea

Of Me

Every year she asks.
I peel off my skin
scour for shortcomings
failures.
Pen to paper before the deadline
when two arms reach for the heavens.
One night makes us new
clean.
This night defines our goodness
our worth.
2024?
What will I feverishly change
reject
in the name of betterment

self-hatred
2023.
Magic came as pain
pain as fog
disguised healing.
So when she asked,
what needs to be fixed?
I know.
It's the part of us that asks such questions
the part of us that is her.
I say,
this year will be hard.
It will require more
more than a year's work
more stillness
more rest
more presence
more silliness
more creativity
more healing
2024?
There will be more.
More for me.
More of me.

Kelsea Guckin

By Phoenix Ríszing
Username: phoenixriszing

Loving Myself More Because If I Don't Who Will?

So there I was, sitting on a twin-sized air mattress on my cousin's bedroom floor in the Bronx—jobless, depressed, and suicidal. It was at that moment that I realized that I was the only person that could save me, so I had to become a Phoenix. I had to spread my wings to fly, or I was sure to die. I've been told my entire life, "You're so strong. You're built for this. You're the strongest person I know." But nobody knows the violence it took to become this gentle.

A little over a year ago, I had an ego death. After months of suicidal thoughts and PTSD flashbacks from my childhood, I mourned, grieved, and rejoiced all within a day. Suddenly, I realized it was destined that way—that I was destined for death and rebirths, so I changed my name to Phoenix

Rîszing. I had to die in order not to die. I had to die in order to become new. I had to let go of the version of myself who was trapped in suffering — allowing myself to grieve various versions of me that no longer served the woman I was becoming.

I spent the majority of my early-mid 20s using drugs and sex to repress my childhood trauma; trauma I didn't even remember having, that was, until I experienced my first PTSD flashback over a year ago. It was a panic attack and bodily flashback episode that brought me back to that seven or eight-year-old little girl who was once molested. That flashback showed me the reality of being a trauma survivor and how easy it is to bury traumatic memories deep within as a way to protect ourselves. Even if we have no recollection of repressing these memories — which I did not, it's no wonder, as an adult, that I attracted a partner who would trigger and mirror my childhood trauma so intensely that it forced me to acknowledge how my childhood trauma led me into a TRAUMA BOND with a toxic partner. The trauma bond eventually led to a new sexual trauma — one that had come to me in a dream as a warning, yet quickly became a premonition and the unfolding of my worst nightmare. My ancestors and my higher self had no choice but to step in, considering that I was running down a road that almost cost me my sanity. I spent all of 2023 processing and recovering from past trauma, but in 2024, I will spend my year LIVING and Loving myself unconditionally and unapologetically. In 2024, I am honoring my needs without guilt. In 2024, I am raising my standards and the price of access to me. I will no longer be offering my body to others in exchange for "love" or validation. In 2024, I will forgive myself for all the things I convinced myself I needed to do in order to survive. In 2024, I will collect memories that remind me why it's a gift to still be alive. I will sit with my inner child and remind her that she is loved, seen, and protected in ways she wasn't all those years ago. We will hold hands and pick flowers, blow bubbles, and daydream about the future that has never looked brighter for us. For the first time in my life, I will choose ME. I'll choose us.

My journey has not been gentle with me, and because of this, I've been forced to address ancestral pain and trauma. It has taken immense courage to sit with this. From an early age, I knew there was heavy darkness in my bloodline, but as an adult, I've been able to break the curse by choosing healing. In 2023, I was called by my ancestors to heal and protect my bloodline through embarking on this journey of healing generational trauma. I had to die and rebirth myself several times. It feels strange to say, but I am thankful for my traumas and my demons. Not because they've given me ANY grace but for volunteering to teach me just how resilient I am. Truth is, I thought I could outrun my trauma until one day it finally tapped me on the shoulder. Now, my trauma and I are becoming one—like lovers in a tub of roses. I now throw roses into the abyss as a way to thank the monsters who didn't succeed in swallowing me alive. This is my offering to my monsters and the version of me that I let die with them. In 2024, I will look in the mirror and tell myself, "I'm proud of you. Thank you for existing" In 2024, I will love myself more because if I don't, who will?

Phoenix Riszing

By Melissa Rodriguez
Username: honeybeeyoself

New Year, New Me

A new year, a new me, what will it be? Longing for change but staying the same. Fighting the wars of fear, failure, self-doubt, procrastination, and no clear path to gratification. Trying to pry the doors of abundance and prosperity open, only to be met by my own self on the other side, keeping them closed tight. This year's goal is to win this fight. To find purpose, to find peace, to find the broken pieces of my dreams. A new year, a new me.

Melissa HB

By Aubrey Schuring
Username: girl_aubrey

———————————

A Proposition To My Future Self

A proposition to my future self:
I will hold myself both accountable and protected
I will stand firm in the earth, barefoot when possible
I will copy song in birds and tend to any garden
I will hold conversation with the neighborhood cat
Slow down to watch the sunrise
The Sunset
I will speed up to meet the stars and run wild to the horses
I will see myself in everything
I will love myself in everything
And I know I will keep burning in everything but
that is something I will finally accept

Aubrey Schuring

By Gabrielle Postlethwaite
Username: gabbypostlethwaite

---

162   # Finally

In the coming new year, I've decided I'm finally going to lose weight. I'll look good and feel great, with a smile on my face. Why? Because I am FINALLY going to lose the weight.

Lose the weight of fear — the fear of trying and worrying about what will happen if I fail. Yeah, I might sink, but what if I sail? Fear will no longer stop me from learning, growing, and becoming more. I know, I know — I might fall. But what if I soar?

This year, I'll lose the weight of responsibility. I know how that sounds, but let me explain. I am hereby no longer responsible when others choose to repeat the cycles of self-inflicted pain. The truth is, I realized I am not responsible for how other people feel, and I only learned that when I decided to break out of my own cycles and finally began to heal. I will learn to set boundaries and see to it that they are respected. I am no longer accepting your terms for my life; consider them rejected.

163

Speaking of feelings and cycles and pain—bitterness tried to take root in my heart, but I've decided to deny its claim. We all have been hurt in this life, something we couldn't stop from coming, but your ashes can't be turned into beauty if you stay angry and unforgiving. So, I'm going to lose the weight of this hurt, which before may have seemed far too daunting, but sometimes just letting go of how you thought things would be can give you the closure you're so desperately wanting. Hurt people hurt people; no one is exempt from that. So, you won't find me on a high horse, pretending I've never stabbed a back. This is what it takes; this is how you heal. I'm dropping the facade; just give me what's real.

I am letting go of the need to always be in control. It's an impossible feat and one that is bound to take its toll. It's laughable, if you think about it, really, and in the words of my baby girl: "No, Mommy, that's silly." I am learning there is beauty in the unknown. A new adventure or an unexpected call from an old friend, life is like a great book, though we don't yet know its end. So, yes, I'm losing the weight of trying to control everything. I'll sit back and enjoy the ride and just let life do its thing.

I think I've made my point; I think you get the gist. Though I have a lot of goals for the new year, losing weight is at the top of my list.

Gabrielle Postlethwaite

By Flannery Joyce
Username: flann199

_____

New Year Goals

New year
New me?
No, not new me
Same me
But with new goals
New goals
New aspirations
Do new things
For the new year
A chance to rest
To restart
To do the things
I said I would

But never did
Last year

It's a new year
So set new goals right
Make new resolutions
Is what everyone says
You do
In the new year
So, what are my goals?
That's a good question
I ask myself
I haven't really thought about it
But I know I should
So goals I want to accomplish
In this new year are:

Getting my driver's license
It's something I should have by now
But I don't
29 with no license
I never really needed it
From living in a city
In a neighborhood
Where I can walk to anything
But now as I get older
I realize I need it

Drinking less
I drink for many reasons
I like the taste
With friends and family
Gives me confidence
Out of boredom
To escape my thoughts
To drink my feelings away
Which is where it gets bad
I know I shouldn't do that
Drink to forget
But I did
I used to
Last year, I tried
To slow down
I was doing good
But had my slip-ups, too
But this year
I want to try it again
Drinking less
And actually accomplishing it
For my family
For my friends
And most importantly
For myself

Focusing on myself
Along with my mental health

167

Such as getting back into yoga
I took classes every weekend
But then stopped
When they filled up
Too fast

Meditating
To help calm down
And to clear my mind
My mind has a million tabs open
It's always fasting
I need to slow down
And focus on myself
Working out more

Climbing
Climbing helps me
Both physically and mentally
It clears my mind
It makes me have to focus
To figure out how to get
To the top
Works my muscles
Legs and arms
I feel it when I stop for a while
Makes me feel stronger
Makes me feel better
Afterwards

It's a challenge
And I love it
I need to climb
More this year
And stop making excuses
For why I can't

169

Journaling
To release my thoughts
My feelings
My emotions
In a better way
A healthier way
Then before
I can't speak
How I feel
But I can write it
How I feel
Writing to let go
Of the darkness
That's inside me

So these are my goals
My goals for the new year
Will I accomplish them all?
I don't know, but I will try to
These goals may be small
Compared to another's

But I don't care
Because these are mine
My goals
To reach
To make
To achieve
In this new year

Flannery Joyce

By K. S. Love
Username: kslove

2024 Figured Out: A Poem

It's 2024.
The welcoming celebrations have ceased.
On my first day back to work,
A coworker asked,
"What do you want for yourself this year?"

I said, "It isn't a matter of what I want,
It's what I need…
There's nothing
I need more than to
free my mind of thoughts
on what I can't do."

She pondered...
Then questioned,
"How will you get to that place?"

"I must embrace fear,
let life run its course,
face challenges head-on and
gracefully excuse myself
from my zone of comfort.

With that, I need to
express gratitude,
take better care of my body, and
value my mental.

Last, I'll build on my knowledge,
smile more often,
act with love, and
work to master the art of patience,"
I declared with great excitement.

"I see you have it all figured out,"
she replied.
"No, I just know what I need,"
I assured her, casually.

By K.S. Love

By Sydnee Cabrera
Username: sydneem

_____

To My New Year

On January 1st, 2024, I found myself making a vision board for the year.

I had done the same last year, and looking back and seeing all that I had accomplished and followed through with gave me closure to the depressive episode I experienced in all 12 months of 2022. I learned to ask for help. I learned to speak up and place fresh soil under my feet to ascend from the hole I had dug for myself. The hole a part of me planned to die in turned into a place for me to plant my feet and give myself flowers.

My flowers have blossomed for this new year and this vision board is going to help me water them.

For the first time in 10 years, I felt connected to a Bible verse. God's and my letters have gotten mixed up in the mail, and I eventually stopped writing to him. I hated what he had put me through and the way he watched me suffer for years, but I realized that in moments when I sat on the floor of my bathroom, unable to breathe, sleeves salty from crying into them, I spoke to him. I wanted someone to listen, and he did, and now I know it's time to break my "no-contact." The night of January 8th, I wrote to him for the first time. I apologized for my absence, explaining why I had been away for so long, and I felt forgiven. In a moment where I expected ridicule and mercilessness, I was forgiven before my ink dried. I want to forgive myself in this way, maybe learn to forgive others the same. I want to heal this year. This is the focus of my vision board. I want to express the kind of love I used to when I was growing up, the unknowing, the unconditional, the innocent. My goal is to close chapters from my childhood that felt unfinished, stories I cannot rewrite for an outcome that better suits who I am today but instead MAKES me who I am.

So, in 2024, I ask God to grant me the serenity to accept the things I cannot change, the courage to change the things I can, and the wisdom to know the difference.

Sydnee Cabrera

By Hannah Gray
Username: hgray624

_____

In This Moment, I Am Grounded

imagine that you are a plant,
tree, shrub, flower,
whatever plant you desire to be,
you are that plant.

your feet are roots,
grounded deep within the earth,
you become one with nature,
peacefully and gracefully growing.

the sun rises casting a warm glow upon you,
wind gently blows through your petals or leaves,
bees and butterflies settle onto you,
such small majestic beings.

you stay grounded,
in awe of the beauty found within nature,
in awe of how the sunshine, grassy plains, mountains, and
bodies of water,
are the most magical of all.

you are present in the moment,
accepting that, you are in fact, a force of nature,
filled with beauty and uniqueness,
character found in each thorn, leaf, petal, or branch.

storms come through from time to time,
however, your roots are planted deeply into earth's crust,
thunder and lightning strike and rumble,
just as the sun shall rise once more.

i ask of you to imagine yourself as a plant,
to stay grounded, present, and most of all,
embrace the fact that—you are a force of nature,
even on the darkest, coldest nights.

i, myself, will do the same.

i will grow in the sunshine,
keep grounded during storms,
be present in the moment,
as each day passes on.

Hannah Gray

By Sarah Ludlum
Username: ludlumpenned

2024 Is The Year I Choose Me

For years, I have chosen everyone else first
I allowed myself to not even be on my own list of priorities
I did not think I deserved to be recognized on my own time
with deserving the merits of love for myself
I had everyone categorized in my mind as more important
than me
I was determined to not be a nuisance or cause anyone
discomfort

2020 changed me as it did others

2020 made me aware of the importance of self stillness
2021 taught me that I do not need to live up to others'
timelines; my own is important

2022 woke up my internal clock of no longer delaying my own growth
2023 broke me of any self-doubt that was leftover of 2022 and set my path on fire
2024 is the year I choose Me

I choose to make myself a top priority on my own list
I choose to make sure I know my worth and my value even when others question me
I choose to be uncomfortable with not taking care of everyone else first
I choose making sure I know I am allowed to love myself honestly and fully
I choose living up to my own expectations and I am looking forward to how this adventure unwinds over this year

2024 is the year I choose me

S. Ludlum

By Cyantha Key
Username: keystone314

_____

Goals for 2024

My goals in the Year 2024,
In the year 2024, the word that comes to mind is simply more.
I want to expand my creativity and explore the depths of
my creative capacity.
I want to write the sonnets and poems etched in my heart.
I want to tell tales from my neighborhood in short stories.
I want to step out of the shadows of doubt and into the light
of hopes and dreams.
I want to make my mark on the world with my own voice
and flair.
I want to be a painter and a poet,
A writer and a thinker,
I want to be a visionary and artist,
An innovator and an dreamer,

In this year, I want to overcome trial and tribulations.
I want the world to know I have a rich imagination.
I want to bring joy and excitement to the minds of the
gallery viewers.
I want to motivate the minds of spectators, and plant joy in
their hearts.
I want to have the courage to say I was brave and bold.
I won't keep my genius stored in my heart,
At the end of this year,
I want the message to be clear,
In 2024,
I will be more,
More braver,
More stronger,
More creative,
More hopeful,
More inspiring,
More bolder,
This year will be a year of more.

Cyantha Key

By Johanna Deletti
Username: jdeletti

_____

May All Your Wildest Dreams Come True

When I imagine you working towards your goals this new year, I see you vividly thriving in competence, pursuit of financial stability and, creating a world for yourself that you have only wildly dreamed of. Thriving in competence will take great focus and determination while learning to become the writer within you. The pursuit of financial stability will take grit to take yourself higher than the Sommelier you deeply dream of letting go. I promise you, my love, there is a second career waiting for you outside the walls of a restaurant and inside your magnificent, ingenious mind. Building on a world for yourself that you have always wildly dreamed of will create a path of confidence and deep understanding of the woman you are yearning to become.

The journey you seek is lit with blazing stars of ideas and deep-rooted desires painted with yellow bricks made of love; you must continue to love yourself through every cutting challenge and every heart-wrenching bad day. As much as it feels like there is no end to start your new beginning, these challenges will only lead you to the greater purpose that you dream of achieving. You will support your every wish with every story you choose to tell, every word you put on paper, and every idea you design from your imagination.

You will travel through foreign countries, speak romance languages with locals, experience cultures outside of your own, and my love, you will produce a life full of magical moments with the man you never knew could love you so deeply. Everything you wildly dream of is waiting to come together in every wild dream you continue to pursue. If you continue to follow the love you have for yourself, the lights will become easier to see and all of your wildest dreams may come true.

I love you, always.

Yours Sincerely,

JD

By Este Masters

Happy New Year

If what they say is true
and you can really be anything
I hope you'll be your own stars and lavender skies
and every phase of every moon

Be your sun that meets the day
Be your air, breath, and fire
Be your lungs that haven't quit

Be the postcard in the mail
on the way to greet old friends
Be your neighbor bringing laughter
and togetherness in cups of tea

Be paintings, puzzles and dreams still left to finish
Be the ladybugs gathered in three

Be every ocean too big to photograph
Be the snapshot from outer space
Be the embers in the backyard woodpile burning
and your midweek coffee date

Be the fireworks and the celebration
Be the rain jumping off concrete
Be the flowers you plant, and more importantly,
Be the roots that no one else sees

Be the first time listening to the song you've been needing
Be the dance class you're scared to take
Be your stumbling and uncertainty
Be every season in its wake

Be the time capsule revisiting every hometown place
you thought surely you outgrew
Be elbows deep in a sink full of dishes
Be the vinyl crackling from the next room

Be open windows and fresh clean sheets
Be the moment to gather your thoughts
Be your voice of grace that says
You are more than "what you ought"

Be summer heat's rest stop for gasoline
Be afternoon's happily snoring dogs
Be the birdhouse in the yard
and the flock of magpies in their waltz

Because if what they say is true
and our lives are up to us
I'd like to think we can be brave enough
to be everything that's been given to us

Este Masters

185

By Jennifer St.Clair (J.St.C.)
Username: jennsaint

———————————

2024: Hours To Goal!

2024: hours to go —
Til the New Year's Party's over and
Aileen leans in to show me a meme, a little dated, about
being sedated by the Ramones:
Twenty, twenty-four hours to go.

That's how this leap year lept in: on word play, a guffaw,
and a grin. And: THAT'S IT!
That's my goal for 2024. That's all. That's it:

To play with words and laugh along to poetry and song,
joke and jape all night long — right or wrong —
With a throng of my favorite people to ring it in with —
Including and increasingly especially always — ME.

Nothing else needs doing or achieving except being. Accept
BEING.
It is my goal that that finally be enough for me.

For, I have spent all the years before 2024 — up to and
including 2023 —
making lists of buckets and wishes of all the things
I need to do or be.

So, new year, new list usually — but NO! — not this!
This time I want only one — okay, maybe a few — things:

To curate and appreciate all that did accumulate before
2024
to make it what it is already about to be.

NO YEAR IS NEW. YET, EVERY YEAR, IT'S TRUE —
We all set out to improve ourselves in the DEAD OF
WINTER

When all the smart mammals are out there staying in:
hibernating
gestating
incubating
investing in their future
by staying asleep — perchance to dream

Of what's soon coming: life and love in store. But they don't start acting on those mores until the actual Spring

So, my only goal for now is to sit back and marvel how I even got here to THIS place and time of being.

It's the start of 2024, and my one and only chore is to see what happens next without expecting a single thing...

Except maybe some more laughs and a few hours left to pass...

Til 2025 has me sedately asking myself the exact same thing.

(Who knows by then what the answer will be?)

J. St. C.

By Victoria Atterberry
Username: vatterberry

Something Special In Me

There's something special in me, but the sheets around me
invite me to lie still.
There's something special in me, but the voice of the newest
drama calls out my name.
There's something special in me, but the hours of scrolling
make it easier to stay put, liking, commenting, and laughing
my precious time away.

As 2024 dawns, I aim to awaken the thing that is special in me.
But not by any unimaginable might nor by any
unprecedented event.
The path to results is simpler than I realize. More
obtainable than the maze my mind has painted, full of
winding paths, convoluted plans, and unforgiving puzzles.

The steps are as follows:
Record the vlog.
Write the story.
Create the choreography.
Master the language.
Learn the instrument.
Love and be loved.

This is the moment I start to create the things I have always wanted to make,
I start to enjoy the things that make my creative spirit sing,
I start to find my rhythm.
I start to find my tempo.

Do not delay, I say. The thing that is special in me grows restless.
And I cannot ignore it any longer.

Victoria Atterberry

By Leah Joy
Username: missjoy121

2024, Provisions And More

My goals for this year?
Mmm, it's not what you'd think.
I'd have to go back and tell you about the time when I was
on the brink
Of a breaking like you've never known.
I will tell a story,
Listen to my tone.
My words will show you something,
That's not typically shown.
It all began in the beginning of this year.
I'll have to admit
by definition I was weird.
But it was actually
Something placed inside of me.

The King of kings began to birth some dreams,
New hopes, visions, and heights I would have never
believed.
I was dead before.
Not in the way you see,
Physical.
Yes, that's happened before
But that's a story for later
When I have time for more.
I was spiritually dying,
A wraith inside
Deathly and decaying
I was on a rapid backslide
Battling a demon, trying to take my life
I was wrecked from the incident with the knife
I started my year in a place
Where I was supposed to heal from it all
And continue to run my race
I turned 18
Still crying the night before
When I should have been
Celebrating that God gave me more
Time when I should not be living anymore.
I knew then, He was still not done
My story wasn't over
It had just begun
And so, as I'm stepping into this next year
His promises will come to pass

those far and wide will hear
And rejoice because God did it again
He slayed my giants
And saved my soul within
Blessings on blessings that's how my new year will began
My potential will unlock and and my dreams will be a
present tense
A life will be made of a pleasing incense
To my Lord, who obliterated my sins and defense.
My goals for this upcoming year
Is living totally free
From the issues of the past that have tried to chain me
Perseverance for my race to be run
And security when I come totally undone
Because let's be real,
trials will come
And try to beat me like the sound of a drum
But with God I beat a beast like you've never believe
And I left it all in the ashes of 2023
2024 is provision and more
I will see come to pass
As I worship my Lord.

Leah

By Ariana Manley
Username: sage

———————————

194

Dear Self, I Will Love You Better.

Dear Self,

I will do love better next time
Starting with me
I will love me better
Wake up in this body
Speak prayer over it
And remember that God
Ordained me worthy
Anointed me with special purpose
Not sacrifice
I will smile wide and full
No longer biting my tongue to keep my truth from falling out
I will love me better

Discontinuing to be confused on my value
Or of what I bring to the table
When I am the home that love is held in
I will lay flowers at my feet
So that the ground is blessed twice
By something sweet
I will love me better
Pour all my effort into my dreams
Instead of into the hands of another
I will love me better
Hold myself gently
when I feel calloused by my own thoughts
when my mind is spiraling with aspects of my ego
I will remind myself that this is part of being human
I will offer myself compassion
when everyone around me has run out of it
I will cup my hands
and whisper kindness into my palms
And place them on my heart until I feel warm again
I will make sure my cup overflows
Make sure to ask no one to fill it
I will be my own mind reader and interpreter
Trusting in myself and not needing someone to invalidate
the doubt in me
I will love myself better
By leaving sticky notes of encouragement on my mirrors
When I feel like I'm slipping
I will grasp whichever limb I need

to keep myself from falling
And even if I fall
I will know that loving myself
means to get back up
And I will get back up
I will make mistakes
But I will love myself enough to learn from them
I will love myself better
To love a lover better
To give and accept love
For love's sake
I will love myself better
Because there's no greater love than the love of oneself
Dear Self,
You are the love of my life.

Ariana Manley / Sage

By Christine Navarrete
Username: chrissywrites

_____

Your Goal Is To Just Be

Dear Me,
You did the work
You trusted the process
Look, I know you, you're going to move on to the next
thing, to finish that next task but might I suggest your goal
is to be present in what you've achieved?
You live in a house of your own
So feel at home
You're feeling a lightness like never before
Step into that freedom
You learned things do work out in the most beautifully
unexpected ways
Keep believing

Happy New Year.

Love,
Me

Chris

By Chrys Takashige
Username: satori

_____

My Ascension

The year to
rise and shine.
"So long" to what was.
"Hello" to what is.
Still thriving.
Thankful to be sustained
by technology and humans
two decades plus.
Time to live more freely.
No cerebral road blocks,
nor abandoning of self.
Marching forward
to where euphoric states await,
in the ocean, on the greens, up on the hills.

200

Returning to acts of love,
from hermit to butterfly,
out and about it shall be.
The dormant right brain
to be awakened
on paper, with rhythms and cuisine.
Moving and grooving
through each day.
Attaining yin-yang status
on the seesaw of life.
The freedom to choose
what is ideal
for the life deserved.
No more compromising.
Forget wasting energy.
Drop the ungrateful.
Evolve into a lightweight
ready to fly and soar
beyond measure.

Chrys Takashige

By Ala
Username: ala

Infinite Power

I don't have resolutions and despite popular belief
I really don't know what I'm doing
Instead, I know more about who I am not
& I know what I will not do.

I WILL NOT WAIT
for anyone or anything to like me
I have no desire to be likable
to the people who see me as debatable
I want to be loved fully and completely
I want to know that I am worth the fight
worth the discomfort
And worth the effort to try to get it right this time.

I WILL NOT LINGER.
on the pain or ambiguity.
part of the awakening / is the awareness /
that everything works out as it should.
there's nothing I can do
there's nothing you can do
there's nothing anyone can do

to keep me from what's mine and
anything 'lost' in the middle is merely practice
to lay my own impatience to rest.

"as I think, so I shall be."
so I let go, consciously
knowing that I will be okay
with the energy of the cosmos leading the way.

I WILL NOT BE AFRAID.
I used to believe that fear was a superpower capable enough
of making me
smarter, sharper, faster,
but I clung to that too much
holding onto that belief until fear crippled me.
// I'm not doing that anymore //
living with fear at the forefront
has made me lose more than its ever made me gain.

last night, I drove to Pahrump
alone at midnight.

it was pitch black out
nothing but mountains for miles and a thousands threats of
danger lined both sides of the roadway.
But I kept driving
I kept going
and I prevailed by repeating that "I am not afraid"
// A new mantra when I start to lose my way. //

I WILL NOT DOUBT MYSELF.
my sacral authority has been strengthened by
18,976 minutes of meditations.
my intuition is more than capable
of interpreting the signs
and synchronicities
embedded within
everything around me.
This is the "Power of Woman"
and all I need to do is listen.

I WILL NOT DEFINE MYSELF BY INSANITY.
I will not repeat the same patterns
and the same behaviors in hopes
of different outcomes.
there is an ebb and flow to everything / the yin and the yang /
perfect pairs that present truths
that I keep persuading myself as wrong.

"Maybe if I try harder, this time it'll be different".
"Maybe this time, they do just need space"
Maybe this. Maybe that.
But maybe not.

These are not chances that I am willing to take
as I gamble my life away.

I will not stay silent.
I will not say "yes" when I mean no
I will not sit by and watch atrocities unfold
when I have a voice.
My boundaries
My emotions
My thoughts
My peace
are all inherently valid and will not be ignored.

This year
I don't have resolutions
and I have no clue what I'm doing
but instead I have this simple equation
where I subtract the distractions
add in new wisdom
multiply the joy
and diving the things I love

to find the real value.
to find the real me
she who already has everything
she needs because she understands her power
and know it lives inside her.

and I hope you can connect to that, too.

ala

By Oswald Perez
Username: opwriter

Looking Ahead To 2024

Dear Unsealers,

It's the halfway point of January. Though I've been taking it a bit slow, I still have plans that I want to achieve in 2024.

I'll tell you what they are…in verse

As 2024 rolls on
Here's what I know…

I hope to expand on my writing gains
With the fourth attempt to bring the next chapter of the Poetic Journey to life
To complete the Tupelo Press 30/30 challenge

Go the distance through NaPoWriMo once again
And possibly, write my next chapter

To make it past my probationary period in February
Seeing in my first anniversary at work full-time come
October

Come the fall, my next destination beckons
As I trade the Aegean for the Adriatic
With visions of being by the sea in Dubrovnik

This is just a taste of the plans in store
Knowing that the rest of this year is open for so much more

Oswald Perez

By Antonieta Paco
Username: priestess_ap

2024 Goals

2024, coming through with a quick arrival to inspire us
furthermore,
made the past look like a blur,
I've collaged many vision boards
and chanted many new resolutions to occur,
I sit here,
saging my manifestations that travel like a smudging smoke,
to close the vision my dreams need to stay afloat,
What are my visions?
I dream big!
my dreams could carry me away like comets in the Universe
or whales in the seas,
my dreams are to travel overseas and visit indigenous
communities,

where their peace treaty has been breached,
my dreams are to help the unhoused, the suffering, and the
innocent,
buy some acres and create more non-profit businesses,
become a farmer who is eminent,
also known as benevolent
A poor girl, a daughter of immigrants,
Using her platform to lessen the homeless crisis and use her
resources to defend communities that has normalized the
act to discriminate,
May every seed I plant below my feet,
be the treasure that we seek,
the soul of the village and the community,
where we share our feed and stories to sing,
as one, the cosmic race,
on the Earth planet we choose to breathe

Antonieta Paco

By Grayson Bell
Username: graysonbbellgmail-com

———————————

Re(solutions): A Poem for 2024

This time
I am
Clawing my way
Out of
The grave
I laid in
The grave
I prayed in
Waiting
For a change
An extricating hand
With a shovel
To come
And dig

Looking for me
Somehow
Knowing I was
In there
The dirt
Never lifted
No matter
How many
Times
I shifted
I would scream
Sometimes
I would even
Sing
Nobody came
I decided
I would
Die in
Darkness
Blind to the power
I could harness
Then I realized
I was awake
Nowhere near
Death
I may have
Felt defeated
But I still

Had some
Strength left
My hands began
To move freely
My legs too
I was never
Stuck
I just accepted
Too many lies
As my truth
Leaving me
Confused
The years
Before
Were heavy
Filled with turmoil
This year is
Brand new
I am no
Longer
Beneath the soil

Grayson Bell

By Ashley Graham
Username: ashleyg9393

———————————

Capable Woman

Dear me,
Yes you.
You are a capable woman. Strong, intelligent, and resilient
is your name. You put fires out that are aimlessly burning,
and in the same breath have the ability to ignite the most
powerful flames.
You are a capable woman: a dog mom, a cheerful wife, and
a spiritual pillar to many. You work hard in everything you
do even when it's not ideal.
You are a capable woman. Allow yourself the time you
need—to heal, to laugh, to cry, and to sigh. Life will always
be busy, but you deserve some rest. Remember, you are
capable, but you are also human.

Oh, capable woman. Please dive into yourself. Make your 30s your best. Let go of the void and shake off the excess stress. Who are we mentally, physically, emotionally & spiritually? Let's find that out. Can we buy out the time to do what we love? Can we live by our rules?

My dear capable woman. This time is yours to spend. Follow your heart and find peace within. Build up yourself the way you desire to be. I believe you can do it. I believe in me.

Love always,

An aspiring capable woman

Ashley Graham

By Camerial Kristen
Username: camerial

Dear 2024

Dear 2024,

I am thrilled to take charge of my life this year! 2024 will be the year of self-love, self-care, and self-growth. To pour into others, I must first pour into myself. So, this year, I will prioritize my needs and honor every part of who I am.

I know that the journey of self-love is challenging, but I am ready to face it head-on. I am determined to become the best version of myself mentally, physically, and spiritually. I acknowledge that there may be bumps along the way, but I will not let them discourage me. Instead, I will use them to show myself how strong I am.

2024 will be a year of transformation, and I can't wait to see all my progress. I am confident that with hard work and dedication, I will achieve my goals and become the best version of myself.

Sincerely,

Made with Love Company, Inc.
111 love street

Camerial Kristen

By LaShae Eaddy
Username: poetrypicasso

———————————

2024

It took your body
Twelve years to climb
Four feet and eleven inches.
Although you have plateaued in figure,
I hope your soul can continue to grow.
I hope your heart expands;
I hope your spirit strengthens;
I hope you can fortify your mind
And feed your passions
A balanced diet.
This is the year
You search beyond:
Beyond yourself,
Beyond the limits you've come to know,

Beyond the 4 ft 11 in at
The top of your head.
I hope you pray deeper;
I hope you love longer;
I hope you work harder;
I hope you play better;
I hope you learn so much
Life starts learning from you.
And while that one
May be just out of reach,
Hopefully,
In 352 days
You'll be used to
Reaching for things
People say are untouchable.

PoetryPicasso

By Sylvia St.Martin
Username: shesgraphic

Clear Vision

Last year, going into the year of 2023, like everyone did when it was trendy, I made a vision board. On that vision board, I said I wanted to make it pink and aesthetically pleasing! With pink being my favorite color and the trendy "aesthetic look" social media is going for nowadays, it was obvious I had to go this route for the look of my board! I continued to search on Pinterest for things I wish to have moving forward in 2023 and made sure to end the search with the phrase "pink aesthetic."

So I pasted my pink aesthetically pleasing Tesla picture to my vision board, my pink aesthetically pleasing image of business packages, and can't forget those pink aesthetically pleasing quotes that I needed on the board or it wouldn't have looked right. The focus of my vision board was centered around looks. It was more important to me how pretty and appealing to the eye I could get it. It did not obtain any depth and there was no vision in the vision. Needless to say, I did not get anything done on that board.

Last year, working on my vision board I really was going about it very superficially— not only a general sense, but also very surface level. I'm certain this is the reason I didn't achieve anything on that board. This year, I'm going about it in a different way, more of a logical approach. I have a clear vision and that vision is to be realistic, that vision is to go deeper and strive to achieve to be that ideal version of myself— not to have the prettiest looking project filled with other people's goals and aspirations that I see on Pinterest. I looked at goals in the sense of what I can reach RIGHT NOW, instead of a step-by-step journey of achievements, opening up new chapters to start and focus on continuously. No more aesthetics, this one is personal!

The way my story was written, my starting point in life didn't give me much leverage. So at times it may seem like all odds are against me. It may seem like what I am reaching for is unrealistic and quite impossible. I read somewhere that, "Holding limiting beliefs become self-fulfilling prophecies." Meaning, if I tell myself a dream is too big for me to achieve and I can't do it, then guess what? I won't be able to do it because I made that decision for my life already before I even started. My starting line does not affect where I will finish, so I believe any dream I dream is obtainable. Goals should be realistic not limited. I do not limit my goals because I find it to be unrealistic. It's actually quite the opposite. I come up with limitless goals and seek realistic ways to go about them.

The vision for my vision board, or in other words, my goals for the 2024 new year is quite simple. I will attract wealth abundantly from multiple different streams of income. I will pass any upcoming tests with perfect scores of 100! This year I am going to start to build credit so that by the end of the year I have a credit score of 750 or higher. That new apartment I've been eyeing? I will reside there, and I will get to and from my place of residence with my new car. By the end of 2024, the new skill(s) I've been working on, I am will be very knowledgeable about and I will work on my projects efficiently. I will seek a better relationship with God because without Him, hard work and determination, and a little bit of manifestation, I will not obtain that ideal version of myself that I know I am capable of being. In 2024 I will be motivated to complete every goal I have for myself and more. I will achieve every goal I set forth with intention.

Sylvia St. Martin

By Leyla Jordan
Username: leylajordann

_____

Broken Up Sunlight

In the era of my second decade,
Entering my most confusing time yet.
Who to be, where to go,
What to do,
Who knows?
I slithered around in fear
Most of 2023.
I crave new skin, I crave brighter days.
I long to give my thoughts action
Instead of letting them
Prance around, dressed in "what ifs".
Chills strike my body at the thought
Of my life being my own.
My palate has become stale

From being stagnant,
Yet I'm afraid of the sours of change.
My feet don't know what direction
To step in but
It's become exhausting
Stepping in fear.
I want this letter, this poem,
To be my step forward.
Still a step in fear
But a step forward.
Refreshed, I am in my era of exposure.
I am in my era of doing.
No longer sitting and wallowing
in anxiety,
Standing up when I feel disrespected.
There is so much more to see, to experience,
to do, to be.
I've grown tired of being the reason
of my own downfall.
Tired of shading
my vision and tainting
My talents,
In fear.
I crave confidence,
I crave a self I've never known.
I crave new skin, I crave brighter days.

Leyla Jordan

By Kelly Lieberman
Username: kelly

Dare To Look This Year

When I am asked what my goal is for this new year, I'd like
to ask a question of my own first;
Have you ever looked into the eyes of a stranger and were
told a story without words?
Have you ever seen the depths of one's heart from a passing
glance?
Eyes tell the truth.
If you dare to look.
Have you ever looked into the eyes of a stranger?
I have.
I've seen unspeakable pain in the eyes of a girl.
A girl whose witnessed the tragedy of addiction overcome
her protector.
Her eyes watched the strong arms of opioids strangle the

one who once gave her life.
She smiles and laughs in the safety of her classroom,
But her eyes tell the truth.
If you dare to look.
I've seen eyes that carry fear.
Fear that has arms and legs and lives in the dark space of
widened pupils,
Waiting to jerk its host,
left and right into isolation,
left and right into depression,
left and right off a cliff.
Fearful eyes are attached to a body of boastfulness.
A body that is big and bad and tough.
A body that if you get too close, it will leave you in the dirt.
Eyes tell the truth, though.
If you dare to look.
If you dare to look in a stranger's eyes,
You might just be daring to save a life.
Because, fellow human,
there are eyes all over the planet that long to be seen.
Their bodies won't show it.
Their mouths won't dare speak it.
But their eyes tell the truth.
The souls of this world are dying.
Dying to be understood.
Dying to be validated.
Dying to be loved.
Dying to be seen.

And when a hurting soul is seen, a hurting soul has a chance to be saved.
So I ask you this;
Do you dare to slow down?
To throw away the typical shiny plastic goals of the new year, in exchange for a life-giving moment?
Do you dare to look into a stranger's eyes?
My goal this year is unlike the rest.
It's to know people.
Love people.
SEE people and help them feel seen.
That's my goal.
With love,
K.

Kelly Lieberman

By Raven Wallace
Username: pinkyravn

Love 1st

The sky is filled with flames tonight
the fire inside can reignite
the ashes fall to the ground
Forever lost not to be found
The person that I was before
Was she not to be adored?
My eyes believed I wanted wealth
My mind would tell me something else
My heart would say there's something more
become the person of your dreams
Tis not easy at it seems

No more goals
No more scores
If loving me is not at the core
No longer opening the door

Raven Wallace

By Roses
Username: roses

_____

New Year Resolutions
Everyone Should Share

Have you ever read the same book but a different story,
there's a saying for that phenomenon
I just finished my Saturday morning coffee and chocolate
chip muffin complemented by my current read
It's that time of the year again Deja Vu
So, I pull out my pen and begin to write about how to
become a better version of you
I didn't fully comprehend what I thought knew
This year I'm going to do something new
Looking in the mirror but only seeing half of me
I lost myself living as person three, instead of the main
character
It's time to take back all of my identity

Completing every goal this year but first let's focus on the top three

Number 1. I'll start by losing weight
Burning the off calories procrastination added
It's easier to run to your goals when you sculpt the weight around your waist
The time is now, why wait
You don't want to be late to your dreams
So, go ahead and book that first trip you've been planning for the last two years

Number 2. I want to travel more
Travel to the past so I can better see my future
A frequent flyer because I was too focused on yesterday
Now these miles are just lessons learned
A frequent flyer because growth is my meditation
If you ever want to get somewhere fast it's better to slow down
Speeding will only get you a $300 ticket you don't have the money for

Number 3. I want to be better financially
Health is wealth or so they say and last year I was broke
Broken heart, shattered mind, but you can still see yourself in a cracked mirror if you choose to
Today I choose you, reciting my daily affirmations
Self-care is one of the best ways to say I love you

Learn to say I do to the future you
Investing in yourself pays more than your 9-5
You will be tired
But that just makes it easier to sleep with your daydreams

Ignore the world the same way they hit snooze
Wake up early, aim high, then reach higher
My goals are only one page turn away
So, stop judging my cover before you read my book
If you simply read the preface, you might begin to
understand the trials I've faced
This book is about the evolution of me
You don't have to read it, but you will respect my art the
same way I cover myself with peace

P.S. these are my goals for leaving 2023…

Roses

231

By Ali Mazza
Username: countertoplovenotes

A Countertop Love Note To Myself

note to self:

stay true to your art
this year. embrace this new month,
january, as

a slab of marble.
you are michelangelo.
use the tools of your

trade to remove its
icy facade: chisel, carve,
sculpt. be relentless

in your pursuit to
create. choose to flip the switch
on your hard hat and
enter the mine of
inspiration daily. dig
for jewels of words, gems

233

of metaphors, and
pearls of wisdom that others
overlook. it's all

there waiting for you,
waiting to be found, unearthed,
and brought to daylight.

yours, in every sense of the word,

ali

By Karina Rodriguez
Username: chickarina

---

234 # Throttles Grip On Life

Throttle and leather gloves, the grip on life I need to make 2024 the year of heart-racing and adrenaline-enticing moments. I put it all on those two wheels: my happiness, mental health, life vision, and social life. At the end of 2024, I wanted to look back at the memories through the miles I put in that odometer. The flashbacks I wanted at the end were of adventure and wind flowing through my long, wavy hair, making the shadow on the road look like flames flowing behind me. The goals for 2024 were placed all on living like it would be my last. Little did I know that on the first day, I set my purpose to live this way, I would feel it all at once: my heart racing faster than the feeling you get after kissing your crush for the first time and adrenaline rushing through my body enough to fuel a group of Marines lining up for a mission. Two wheels became warm and cushiony angel wings wrapped around my trembling body. The wind in my hair was found flowing all around my falling body because I had none in me for a few seconds; just like that, flashbacks came to me of all the people I'd never see again if the tumbling didn't stop. My odometer stopped, but my mind raced, and it raced faster than ever before, replaying all of the moments in life that made it all worth living up until this point. The grip I had on the throttle was gone, lost it all, it was it; this is where my grip on life came to a literal end, or at least I thought. Tumbling, sliding, and flying through the handlebars, the only goal I had was to live one more day. This couldn't be it; the day I pledged to live like it was my last was not the day I wanted it all to end. When it all stopped and became still, I realized I lost grip but I gained a second chance at gripping onto him, the one who kept me safe, taught me the throttle and gave me my smile back. 2024 took me on a tumble on day one but gave me one more day to get up off the wet, muddy grass and give my favorite person a hug.

Chickarina Rodriguez

By Janet Joshuan
Username: jjoshua

I'm Doing That!

Eyes open and there's my smile.
I'm alive and I made it.
Lord, thank you for seeing me through.
12 more months to create internal joy and more self-love.
I'm doing that!

Is that the sun shining ?
Sure as hell is, and it's 2024.
Clap clap because, It's about to go down.
12 more months to create financial abundance.
I'm doing that!

Alexa play Anita Baker, "You Bring Me Joy!"
Who is that dancing in the window?

It's me, because I bring me joy.
12 more months to create that solo dance performance.
I'm doing that!

Shit!
Your son is getting married in 4 months.
You heard me, 4 months!
Weight Watchers app, can I get a clap
Clap?
4 more months to look extra good and 8 more months to
feel like I'm Hollywood!
I'm doing that!

The journal is open to create more stories.
Traveling more to see what else is in store.
You wrote a story from the heart in 15 minutes and won
that contest.
Shut up! Who did that?
12 more months to dedicate time to writing, reading and
expressing.
Yes, you!
I'm doing that!

Don't you think you're doing a lot?
What?? One son overcame his panic attacks, stuttering and
is 29, a plumber and getting married.
The other son overcame having seizures and couldn't talk
for almost a year and has graduated music school and has

an internship as an audio engineer.
Dam right I'm doing a lot, cause I'm doing all of that!

Janet Joshua

By Abigail Stopka
Username: astopka811

_____

2024 Goals, A Symphony Of Love

In the dawn of 2024, a canvas unfurls,
With goals profound, like precious pearls.
Self-love, like a compass, guiding my way,
In the gentle embrace of a brand-new day.

Within, I seek a love so deep,
A promise to myself, a secret to keep.
Mirror reflections, it is a start,
Loving every piece of me, a work of art.

In the tapestry of dreams, a vow I weave,
To embrace imperfections and in them, believe.
Stars in my soul, twinkling bright,
I continue on this journey of self-love's light.

Acceptance, the bridge, to hearts that care,
In 2024, love is in the air.
No fortress of doubt, no walls to build,
A dance with hearts, the space is filled.

With open arms, I welcome the tides,
Affection and warmth in love's sweet strides.
In this chapter, I choose to receive,
Love's symphony, in which to believe.

Nurturing my mind, a garden of thought,
Seeds of wisdom, lessons sought.
Books and knowledge, like rain on soil,
A fertile mind, a lifetime to uncoil.

Learning and growing, expanding my view,
In the vast expanse of the intellectual brew.
A sanctuary of thoughts, a haven of peace,
Nurturing my mind, the quest shall not cease.

2024, a year of growth and bloom,
A tapestry woven with lessons from the gloom.
In self-love's embrace, I find my might,
Accepting love, like morning light.

Nurturing my mind, a scholar's quest,
In the pages of wisdom, I am truly blessed.

The mind, a garden, thoughts take flight,
In the canvas of dreams, I find my light.

So here's to my 2024 journey, a story to tell,
In the symphony of life, where dreams swell.
I set my intentions, a heartfelt decree,
For a year of love, growth, and wisdom, to be.

Abigail J. Stopka

By Nysha Lee
Username: nyshacamilo

My Best Me

And like that 2023 is over, this year flew by
But isn't that what we say every year when the end is near?
Still though time does seem to speed up annually
Does that come with age?
I'm only 23, a 2000's baby is what I be
Last year I finally learned to love me
That along with a lot of other things
Habits are hard to change especially when taught young
Negative habits were all I knew
Being toxic unconsciously, wanting control over everything,
vices to "keep" the pain away

Smoking, drinking, eating, sexing
All fake distractions that in the end, made me worse

Trust issues
But I called it individuality
The inability to listen, being stubborn and hardheaded
2024 I realize, accept, and input the facts that help me grow
It's okay to listen, be silent, intake, and think
Not everyone is out to hurt me

Balance and confidence are needed to not take everything
personally
Are you a reflection or a lesson?
I go to my therapist for a session
I need to release and let go
So that way I won't feel so low

2024 is where I meet sober me and face everything inside
The world is proving what's in the dark must always come
to light
But I, by myself choose whether I win that fight
To face and to conquer
Or to ignore and ignore and ignore until I blow up

Physically I must strengthen myself
When I do something I don't want to do that strengthens
my mind
When I strengthen my mind I have the ability to do
anything I want
So I wake up early, work out, no eating until noon

At 7 I stop eating, meditate and give thanks to the moon
The moon illuminates my battles

Battles that no one can fight for me
I, by myself must choose my destiny
And I choose to first change my melody
From darkness to light

From anger to forgiveness
From sadness to happiness
From negativity to positivity
From irritability to patience
From assuming to asking
From quiet to loud, confidently and unapologetically

From changing my melody I attract what is meant for me
From changing my melody I can accept and maintain all
that is for me

2024 is my year of love, light, success and peace
2024 is the year meant for my best me

Nysha Lee

By Alessandra Suchodolski
Username: thegratefulmindbodycoachgmail-com

Chronic Pain No Longer Controls Me

I've always wanted a career where I can help people.
In 2023, I discovered my true calling, and received my
certification in Integrative MindBody Coaching. This year,
my focus is on sharing my story and expanding my business,
so that I can help other people with chronic pain on their
healing journeys. My chronic pain journey is as follows:

At the end of 2020 and into early 2021, I had the incredible
opportunity of backpacking across Europe for three months.
I explored the beautiful countries of England, Ireland,
Northern Ireland, Austria, Switzerland, and Italy. It was
a once-in-a-lifetime trip, and I am so thankful for the
wonderful people I met, and the amazing experiences that I
will always remember.

Six months after returning to the U.S., I became incredibly ill. Curled up on the couch and in excruciating pain, my life froze to a standstill, as did most of the world due to COVID. Doctors diagnosed me with Irritable Bowel Syndrome, which is a fancy way of saying "we don't really know what's wrong with your digestive tract, but it's not functioning properly". In January 2022, I was diagnosed with Crohn's Disease.

Doctors immediately put me on steroids to help calm down the inflammation in my digestive tract. Although it was a "mild steroid," my body reacted horribly to the drug: I had uncontrollable hunger that could not be satiated, no matter how much I ate; I developed really bad acne on my face; my hair started to fall out; and I even went into a dissociative state. Based on the advice of my pharmacist, I was able to slowly wean off the steroids. The next drug that doctors wanted to put me on was in the same class as a drug that I was allergic to. When I went to pick it up, the pharmacist at the counter warned me that if I had a bad reaction I could die.

At this point, I was done. I was over doctors running countless tests on me (I had my blood drawn ten times that year alone!), and fed up with medication that only made me sicker. But, I wasn't ready to give up. I have always been a fighter, so if there was a way to limit or even reduce the inflammation in my gut, then I was going to unlock the secret! It was then that I decided to take a more natural approach to healing my body.

Receiving acupuncture treatments, every week, was the first big leap in my healing journey. I was skeptical at first, but after just one session I had more energy than I had had in the past year, and my pain levels were significantly reduced. As someone who has personal experience with Irritable Bowel Disease, my acupuncturist also recommended some supplements I could try, in order to bring down my inflammation levels. I am so thankful to have her in my life, because she has been such an incredible resource to keep me healthy, no matter what is going on with my body.

My pharmacist also told me about the Autoimmune Protocol diet. By cutting out all types of inflammatory foods, I was able to significantly decrease my pain. After a while of being on that diet, I was even able to add some foods back into my meals that I knew didn't bother me. I now follow the Paleo Diet, with the exception of nightshade vegetables.

Long term use of NSAIDs can cause ulcers, which make digestive issues worse. I am lucky to live in a state where cannabis is legal. I used THCa, which is derived from hemp, and the precursor to THC, in order to further control my pain levels. What I love about THCa is that it directly reduces inflammation in the digestive tract without getting you high!

January 2023, I got really sick again. I went to the emergency room, and am so grateful to the staff for running full diagnostic testing. When you have a chronic illness, oftentimes doctors will dismiss your symptoms as your disease. After all these years of being told I had Crohn's Disease, it turns out that doctors had incorrectly diagnosed me. I actually had a bacterial infection, which is found in unpasteurized dairy in northern Europe, that causes inflammation in the same part of the gut as Crohn's. Doctors gave me an antibiotic that finally got rid of the bacteria.

Although my inflammation levels are back to normal, I still have chronic pain. I hope that my story inspires other people, who become unexpectedly sick, after traveling, to get tested for bacterial and parasitic infections. In 2024, I also hope to help others with chronic pain, live fuller and happier lives, by offering them support through life coaching.

Alessandra Suchodolski

By Antoinette Gonzalez
Username: @algonzalez

2024

2024 — New Year, New Me!
You know the same thing we ALWAYS say!
What makes this year so different?
My levels of Effs to give.
I'm walking into 2024 with full knowledge,
I will became the villain in a lot of peoples reality.
Honestly, that makes me feel content
Because that means I'm becoming the hero I deserve to be
in my reality.
Look, it's a bird, it's a plane,
Nah — its Antoinette taking her power back.
I'm a mom, daughter, wife, friend and the list goes on
But most importantly — I AM ME!

I have been in a cocoon; realizing I'm embarking on an evolution.
I'm excited to spread my beautifully-crafted wings wide and proudly!
My wings will bring boundaries that will lead to a limitless life!
My wings will gift me a little blue book.
My little blue book of adventure and memories!
I will break the chains placed on me from generations past.
Setting my bloodline free —
By betting on me!

AL Gonzalez

By Vicki Trusselli
Username: vickitrusselliart

_____

My Subtle, But Important 2024 Goals

Dear Unsealed,

My goals for 2024 are somewhat different that in 1990 or 2007. I am 74 years old. I know my goals are different apparently because I am older and the fact I survived long covid and the effects on my body and major surgery. I almost died in April 2022. However, I am alive. I am a Virgo, Leo moon rising, born on the cusp of Libra. I shall talk about more subtle goals than I would have at 20, 30, 40, 50, or 60. My goals are:
1. To remain as healthy as possible.
2. To remain alive.
3. To continue my freelance writing and photography.

4. To continue to spread love and light.

5. To perhaps make a little extra money to help with bills.

6. To always see my doctor.

7. To continue my gluten-free, lactose-free diet as much as possible.

8. To walk more, swim if the weather permits.

9. To continue my meditation practices.

10. To analyze what I am doing and what another person means with their words as they speak to me or other people.

11. To cut back on clothes, and shoe spending on Wish and Temu.

12. Be kind but not vulnerable the full 12 months of 2024.

I will wake up every morning to the sound of music playing through Google Mini or Alexa. I will remember my vivid dreams of people, places, things to write down the specifics of my dreams to create stories of inspiration, but to not forget that inspiration is a part of a negative experience to be brought out into the light. I will take care of my health and continue to think young. I will continue my political activist positions regarding human rights, women's rights, LBGTQ rights, voting rights and democracy for all.

My goal to spread light, love and peace may sound repetitive to some people, but to me it is my most important goal for 2024 and beyond. Without peace, love, and light there would be continuous wars and evil wrongdoing in our society. So, there needs to be more people involved in this goal. Equality and human rights are not political as they are a humanitarian society procedure.

I will spread light and love through my writing and photography with periodic checks of analyzing the good, the bad, and the ugly in all facets of life on Earth.

Sincerely,

Vicki Lawana Trusselli
December 21, 2023

253

Vicki Lawana Trusselli

By Ricardo Albertorio
Username: gorilladna

_____

New Year Resolve

Living in shadows of my past

Roaming hallways of my mind

Afraid to turn corners too fast

And the memories I would find

Resolved to pause and change my stance

And shake the past's dust off my shoes

I will give next year a chance

To see in color instead of blues

Those old walls become withdrawn

As fresh grass grows beneath my feet

This old year has come and gone

My new self I prepare to meet

This New Year I have a choice

My liberty comes with it's dawn

A small change in my mind's voice

To a positive antiphon

My New Year's dreams are made of light

Washing tears and sorrow away

All I did was adjust my sight

To view a better, brighter day

Ricardo Albertorio

By Hirasoul
Username: hirasoul

Bestseller

Number one or number ten
I just want to win
Something.
I guess something real.
2024
I want feel
ALIVE
I want to heal
MY MIND.
I'll write the novel
Type the memoir
Scribble the essay till my knuckles bleed.
I'd be sincere
Finally free, awake and clear.

Momentary Success will Finally be consistent.
One day,
In 2024
I'll be the bestseller
In the NY Times
For trying times
Without wasting time.
So what will I achieve?
Who will I be?
My new goal is to speak
Factually
With intent
I'll no longer accept
Maybe's, wait's, or let's see.
I'm achieving what God intended for me
Happiness
Wonder
Success
Laughter.
The world will understand what I can do.
Mediocre or strange,
I'll stand on my truth
Against every hurricane
Every opinion
And every rotten tomato.
2024 I'll overachieve
Whether 1 million hear my story
Or only 15 read.

My fulfillment won't come from the awards
Or the recognition.
I'll be a bestseller
Because for the first time
In the history of my life
My heart spoke
And my mind Listened.

Hirasoul

By Aimee Concepcion
Username: aimeev

Let My Fire Burn

Your fire is what I admire, what I desire. You light a fire in my soul and fill the bowl in my chest with passion my mind can't even ration. I must be in a daze or maze, trying to run and hide but every corner I turn your fire still burns. I crash into wall after wall getting burned and even then I wouldn't want to return. Because a life without passion is something most people lack in. Even if you burn me to ashes and leave me with unhealed gashes I would still run into your maze, even on my saddest of days. I hope you never lose your fire and allow it to burn bright even on the darkest of nights, when you wanna give up the fight. Because once you start to touch people with that flame it'll catch like match, batch after batch and soon the whole world will be on fire just like the girl I've always admired.

Aimeevc

By Rebecca Engle
Username: rengle3

_____

Stepping Stones

Embarking on my journey, through graduate school
teaching is where I find my passion.
Obtaining that teaching certification I aspire to lead the way
Guiding and shaping minds no matter what challenges may
come our way.

Within the classrooms I will eagerly share my knowledge
Assisting children in their learning process and nurturing
their growth.
Designing lessons that ignite their curiosity and enthusiasm
Transforming education into an joyful experience.

My business is akin to a blossoming flower
I will nurture it with care. Watch it flourish.

Creating crafts that radiate beauty,
Bringing joy to others and making them uniquely mine.

Undoubtedly obstacles will cross my path
I will confront them with unwavering determination.
This year my dreams will soar above
As I strive towards achieving my goals with might.

Thus stepping into this chapter of life
Embracing aspirations, with a fiery passion.
Remarkable accomplishments lie on the horizon
Let us make each day bright and sunshiny in this year

Rebecca A Engle

By Jaselynn Villalpando
Username: Jaselynn

_____

The Year Of Present Moments

Often when we think of a New Year resolution or New Year goals for the upcoming year, we usually have a big goal we want to accomplish like getting a new job, getting a new house, meeting a partner if we are single, having a child, or buying a new car. But what if we were to change our mindset and also see smaller goals just as big as the big ones?

This upcoming year, I am dedicating myself to looking forward to the smaller things like finding peace, doing the things that make my heart feel whole — like sharing a laugh with loved ones, taking a walk outside and breathing the fresh air, or maybe even making time for a hobby that I neglected due to being so busy with work and my personal life.

My ultimate goal for next year is to be PRESENT. Life is often so fast-paced that sometimes we may forget to be present in the moment and take every moment in. I want to be present in everything that I do. Even the simplest things, like cooking a meal and sharing a meal with friends or family or even by myself. I want to take the time to do things that make me feel a spark, like writing a poem, reading a book, and meditating with music, which makes the soul feel good.

Although I want to continue to blossom in my career as a Marketing Specialist and I want my business to blossom, most of all, I want to continue to grow into the person that I am meant to be and continue to find my purpose. The person that I am right now, at this moment, writing this letter about what I am most excited about for the next year, will be a different person reading this at the same time next year, which is why I am so focused on being present every day. I am excited to see the Woman that I am going to become next year and the peace I will continue to find in myself and my loved ones. The laughs I will be able to share with loved ones. The meals I will be able to eat. The new people I am going to meet. I am most excited to see my life change, transform, and prosper. I am so excited to see how much my relationship with God is going to flourish. Every year, there is a new version of myself; I am never the same person each year. I go through joy and pain, different transformations that make me a wiser person.

Next year I dedicate time for myself to find a spark in me that I never knew I had, to move and flow through life with good intentions, better environments, intentional friendships, intellectual individuals, creative people, broken people, and joyful people. I want to take every negative and turn it into a positive and have more faith over fear.

This upcoming year, I am dedicating myself to nourishing who I am, loving who I am, being present, sitting with myself, appreciating everything that I have, and never taking a second for granted. Perhaps when you are reading this, it may seem like a personal letter to myself, maybe it seems to fit more to my future self than what I am most excited about, but this past year was a year of self-realization that happened at the speed of light. So, this upcoming year, I am most excited to live in the PRESENT moment every day.

Cheers to a year of living in the present moments!!

Jaselynn Villalpando

By Vision Woodall
Username: vizo2123

Joy

Endless Smiles
Heart unbroken
Life looking up for you
Looking at the girl of your dreams
Doing what you love
Writing more
It's your passion
Spread your voice
Let them hear you
It's okay
Don't be scared anymore
To let it show how talented you are
Express
I'm sure it'll have them impressed

But again you're not doing it for them
You write for you
It brings such joy
Puts an instant smile on your face
Let's Embrace
No more hiding in the shadows
This is our year to show who we really are
Not what others want to believe
Protect your peace
Go with the flow
Let it be
We are truly smiling again

Vision W.

By Cherie
Username: cherthing

New Flowers

Another year down this road
In many ways I've grown
Spontaneity, once my greatest fear
A trip into the unknown

I'll stop seeing my body as a prison
A cage that I can't escape
For this "prison" has fought many fights
And is still fighting until this day

I'll view the world with a little less fear
And give open doors a chance
Tomorrow isn't promised
So I'll make every moment last

I'll tend to my own garden
Watering the field in which I lay
No more searching for greener pastures
Just staying in my lane

The spring will bring new flowers
The weeds may still arise
I'll nip all problems in the bud
I'll no longer keep them inside

I'll be a better person
I'll learn from my mistakes
I'm not as lost as I once was
Maybe this year I will find my way

Cherie Matzen

YOUR PERFECT DAY

By Kortney R. Garwood
Username: kortkort

A Perfect Day
For A Perfect Me

This day starts with me opening my eyes to give thanks.
Thanks to My King, My God, for soothing my soul.
Allowing me to wake up in absolute peace and feel whole.
I feel as though I'm lying in the clouds,
emotionally safe and secure as I embrace this moment.
This is my state of euphoria, and I emphatically own it.
My mind methodically plans for what lies ahead
as the lyrics to melodic tunes play in my head.
My perfect day has just begun.

The routine of my day has never been so smooth
I patiently take my time constructing my look to fit my mood
From head to toe...
My glow, my fit, my flow.

I look in the mirror, pleased with what I see,
comfortable in my skin and free to be me.

As I head out into the world and follow my script
I long for the taste of some java, retail therapy, and a
favorite flick
Why? These are the makings of me.
The smile on my face and the confidence in my walk.
I could live out this day many times over.
No stress, no strife, no roadblocks ahead.
My perfect day is far from over.

273

This day is just what I've made it
with the blessings I've been given.
The strength to get up and live my life.
The mindset to understand that life is what I make it.
The love that I have for myself to do the things that make
me happy.
Most of all, knowing that every day is a gift
and not to be taken lightly.

As the evening rolls in and slows down my perfect day,
I pull up a seat at my favorite speakeasy without dismay.
There to indulge, I partake in a lovely, herbaceous and tart,
yet ever-so-sweet libation,
as I wait for this day to deliver its final culmination.
Not sad to see it go by any means,
because I know there will be many more days like this to be seen.

Perfect in every way.
Just me living, loving, and enjoying my fulfilling day.

While reminiscing about this day, I sit back and say...
There was nothing particularly special.
Nothing out of the ordinary.
Just a day of me doing me.
I suppose that's what makes it so perfect,
it reminds me to just be.
A perfect day, for a perfect me

Kortney R. Garwood

By Kalianah Wogoman
Username: kalianah

───────────

Man, What A Day...

What would a perfect day look like to me?
What a great question
I guess it would be to break entirely free,
From this cursed nightmare called 'people pleasing'.
It would be me waking up and not despising the outcome
of each day
Man, that would be euphoric
I can see it now, painted like this
A cool, refreshing breeze flowing through my long brown hair
Whispering inspirational ideas in my ear
I would actually be me, who I was meant to be.
And not being scared to be free
My life to be more than just me
I want to be a part of something bigger,

Like setting others free
Breaking them free from their burdens,
Their shame, Their guilt... Regret.
Helping them overcome trials against them
But in order to do that, I have to break free myself
So I wouldn't be fooling anyone with my frauded hypocrisy
My perfect day would consist of these things,
Not blinded by favoritism, helping those in need
Breaking shackles off of people's burdened feet
Setting all of Lifes' captives free
It starts with me
I will fight to win this perfect day
For it catapults me to be the woman I strive to be
I want to feel victories wind breeze past me
As I run in this journey of self-love
The day of perfection, I will be
Bold, I won't cower to the bullies in life that antagonize me
Courageous, I won't hesitate to do what's right
Brave, I will do what is needed for my peace
Loving, I won't let bitterness ruin my integrity
Happy, I won't let others steal my joy
Kind, I will not stop treating everyone with respect
Discreet, I will only open up to those I trust
Discerning, I will know who to trust
I will be strong.
So that I won't let others steam roll over me
Truly let their remarks, roll of my back
I will be completely unbothered by the negative words

Only spewed to hurt me, or to control me
I am not their puppet, not even my own
I will be the woman who is dignified and walks in grace,
But I will be bold and stand my ground unafraid.
I will make choices that benefit me, and those who love me
I will no longer make sacrifices to those who only hate me
Man, what a day
I will wake up, day in and day out
Putting on my game face, and my war paint
Wielding my shield that was meant to protect
Fearlessly charging with unwavering Faith
But, something seems off, what is it?
I can feel it in my bones.
I look down at my hip, and had a realization
I have a sheath, what is that I see?
I dusted off my sword, which waited for me patiently
I finally use it to combat the things trying to hurt me
Which each swipe, I break my own shackles free
So that I can be the me that I was meant to be
To me, that would be the perfect day,
The first day of the rest of my life.
That pining for freedom turning into my reality
That would catapult me into my destiny
Each step with liberty
Pure joy
Loving myself
So I can truly love others

Man, what a day
What a perfect day.

Kalianah

By Necia Campbell
Username: vermontpoetess

_____

Mason

My day could start in ashen gray
like dried-up winter weed bouquets,
but then my grandson shrieks, "Mammay!"
and color swirls in rich array.

A fingerpainted masterpiece
infused with snacks and sweetened tea—
bright backdrop for the tales we read,
immersed in toddler fantasy.

Flamboyant toys conceal the floor,
confetti from a plastic war
that ranged from couch to Singapore—
and now he begs to go outdoors.

Bemusement stains pale cherub cheeks
and nature springs delighted shrieks
when stones splash into frothy creeks
or bluebird skies frame honking geese.

Aweary fingers grab my hand,
for will alone cannot withstand
the golden grains of sleepy sand;
I lull him into lala land.

Reflection on this drowsing dear
who celebrates with heartfelt cheer
the wonderment of Gaia's sphere
is every dark mood's rainbow cure.

Necia Campbell

By Rebecca Engle
Username: rengle3

Imperfectly Perfect

We chase the dream of a perfect day,
But imperfections won't go away.
In this world of chaos, we stumble and sway,
Yet beauty hides in the mess we create.

Laughter echoes, but tears fall too,
In every hello, there is a goodbye too.
The sun shines bright, but my shadows loom,
In every moment, a story's hidden gloom.

We quest for control, but life's untamed,
Unpredictable twists and turns we can't reclaim.
Yet in the midst of turmoil, we find our strength,
A resilience that guides us through life's length.

So let's embrace the journey, with all its flaws,
And find the beauty in the imperfect laws.
For life's not about seeking perfection's gleam,
But dancing with the mess, and making it our theme.

In the uncontrolled moments, we find our voice,
A unique melody that echoes our own voice.
The same melody that makes us make a choice.
Let's cherish the imperfections, the quirks and the flaws,
For they shape our story, and make our life pause.

Rebecca Engle

By Ricardo Albertorio
Username: gorilladna

Sun-Settle

Sunset comes in muted hues

Orange fire and baby blues

Seaside skies, so vast in views

Birds pass lovers, two by twos

The day erased to bygone news

Sunlight fades to starry muse

Gentle flames from bonfires fuse

Bring restful bliss from daytime's ruse

From sunrise lies to nighttime truths

Our life resets when dawn renews

Ricardo Albertorio

By Jovon Reed
Username: vonj

_____

P. R.A.Y

I've been going through some things…

I had a dream, it was something like Dr. Kings.
I had a dream, it was something like Dr. Kings
But I aint have the answers Sway, so I went somewhere and prayed.

I pray one day we all take the time out to read, so our minds will be set free. Slow down and end the programming of the music & the T.V.

I pray we become more conscious of the things we consume, redefine what we call food.
I pray we learn to nourish our mind, body & soul.

I pray one day as a people we become whole.
I pray one day, as brothers and sisters we can tend and
mend each other's broken wings.
I pray we can learn to do things from our heart, and not just
to be seen.

286

I pray we truly believe we can fly! Without a basketball,
backwood, sheets and funnel or whatever method it is you
use to get high.

I pray we stop living just to get by.
I pray we use our voices to sing to the most high.
I pray we look in the mirror, acknowledge and turn from
our wicked behavior. For let a man examine himself.

I pray we stop bragging about riches and strive for wealth.
I pray we stop playing the game for self, the only way to win
is to not even play.
I pray we all can sit and learn to pray.

I'm not a player, I'm a prayer.
I pray that those who think they have to keep it on them,
pray that they never have to use it. It's a war within
ourselves and some things I pray we can learn to leave on
the shelves and at the altar.

I pray we unlearn all the detrimental things they've taught us.
I pray we realize it's a spiritual war for our souls, and that

it's all mental.
I pray we realize that sex is sacred, and learn to respect our temples.
I pray that when it gets dark, you can be light for your peers.
I pray that this prayer falls on open ears.
I pray we all learn to face our fears.

I pray we can acknowledge each other by name.
I pray that you recognize, I am you and you are me. We're one in the same.
I pray we learn to hate fame. I pray that your spirit is renewed. Realizing you're a fearless, righteous, educated and strong human. That's F.R.E.S.H.

I pray you know you're not lucky. But yes, you are blessed.
And yes, I pray this prayer outlives me.
I pray you share and soak up all of this knowledge and wisdom I've given from my heart for free. Amen

Jovon Reed

By Tracy Barnes
Username: poeticaddiction_365

288 # My Perfection

As close to perfection
A day can get
It has to be filled with
Joy, laughter and a good time
Simplicity at its finest
I picture a day filled with love
Surprising my Bae with tickets
To see one of her favorite comedians
B. Simone
Not ruining the surprise
Being a little suspenseful
'Cause the romance
Should never die
Keeping the spark alive

Laughing uncontrollably
From start to finish
Seeing that smile on her face
Means so much
Any day with you makes the world
Seem perfect
Even though we know that not to be true
You are quite a dream come true
Any other day that could even measure up
Would have to be filled with
Rest, relaxation, some good music and poetry
A warm bubble bath to soothe the tense muscles
Forgetting the troubles of the day or week
Allowing my self-care to be my peace
Resetting my intentions
Cleansing my mind, body and spirit
A perfect day can lead to many blessings
I just pray for a day that is calm
That leads to memories to be cherished
And is close to my definition of perfection!

Tracy Barnes

By Jody Seymour
Username: seymojl

A Perfectly Perfect Day

Streaks of gold sift through the slits of wood as I wake to feel the warmth caress my face.

Lips brushing against my forehead with silken kisses gently encouraging me to open my eyes.

A quiet conversation while slowly sipping cinnamon tea. I feel the heat in the curve of my hand as it transfers from my favorite ceramic mug.

Bringing me peace as I embrace the tranquility of the moment. The aroma enveloping my senses and perfuming the room.

I casually let my fingers slide over my wardrobe as I create my ensemble for the day.

The beauty of feeling unhurried and able to relish in the pleasure of selecting garments showcasing my individuality.

I fold my body into my girl, a brilliant blue Jeep, made naked as to relish the scents of spring and the whispers of the wind.

The destination not the priority. A leisurely excursion to escape the restlessness.

Taking in the warm breeze on a sunny afternoon.
The radio playing my favorite songs, bringing back memories of times past.

The path followed as I sail through the countryside leaving thoughts of my younger years and dreams left along the way.

Stopping midday at a favorite cafe to indulge in a meal with my closest friend.

The conversation bringing joy to my soul as we talk lightly and laugh loudly without reservation.

Smiling as I head back home with the hours on the backside of the day. Time moving slowly and shadows appearing as the miles drift by.

I lace my shoes and head out into nature to indulge in the solitude of running alone. This too invoking feelings of pure satisfaction.

Allowing for silent meditation and a chance to release the burdens held within. The one true moment of peace as I feel the calmness radiating throughout my body.

As day cascades into night I welcome the quiet of the evening with the one I hold dear.

Welcomed home with a sweet embrace. The beauty of detailing our day in an encouraging exchange.

The sun slowly fading and capturing the last remnants of this beautiful moment in time.

I climb into the comfort of our bed with the arms of my beloved pulling me near.

I drift off knowing I wouldn't change a thing. Time stands still as I recall the perfect day.

Jody Seymour

By Hannah Gray
Username: hgray624

———————————

Sunshine Psyche

one day it's dark,
actually, it's been dark, for months,
so dark that one could not see in front of them.

however now—
now, there is light.

at the flip of a switch what was once dark—is bright.

the gloomy cloud has passed,
the rain has stopped,
beautiful rainbows begin to appear.

sunlight glistens over the waterfront,
sunlight that makes brown eyes turn to honey,
warmth of light that gives you hope,
fills you full of glee.

the shadows hide away,
the light is beaming,
i can see again,
i can slow down.

i can feel positivity in all that surrounds me.

beauty is in this life,
beauty is all around.

skies turn to cotton candy,
lovers turn to home.

no longer lost,
everything i have longed for,
lays before me.

i see clearly again.

this is who i am.

i am the sunshine,
the light,
the gleeful warmth.

the switch flipped,
my light is now on,
newfound growth shines from within,
creating greater hope for tomorrow.

Hannah Gray

By Jamell Crouthers
Username: aquarianmelo

A Beautiful Day In Nature

We always get asked what's your ideal "perfect day,"
As I've gotten older, it's changed in so many ways.
The place I'm at in my life, it's very simplistic,
Especially since I've grown, aged and learned so much
about myself.
A perfect day for me is actually by myself,
It's an every Friday thing that I always do.
Waking up to sun shining bright through my window,
As I open the shades in my apartment to embrace nature.
I start my day drinking warm water to open my stomach,
Then making myself a good breakfast which consists of
waffles, a muffin and fruit.
Next comes stretching my body and packing my bag,
To venture out into the world, embrace and appreciate nature.

I put on my helmet, put on my earplugs, put my backpack
on my back,
Hopping on my bike to go on a nice bike ride through my
neighborhood.
As I ride my bike and cross streets, I'm appreciating the
sunlight hitting my skin,
As my eyes look at the world from behind my sunglasses,
I look at the mountains as it becomes beautiful scenery,
Making my way to a long bike path to get a few miles in.
The music playing can be anything from hip-hop to lofi music,
Most of the time, it's a playlist I created where I don't skip songs.
There are people on the path walking or biking, sometimes
it's a good morning,
Most times, it's just me being in the moment and thinking
about nothing.
After three miles, it's off to the basketball court,
To get a workout in where it's me, my basketball and the rim.
For an hour and a half, it's working out, people watching
and listening to music,
There isn't a care in the world, no lists to do, no phone calls,
No social media, no text messages, my world is quiet.
After a workout, it's resting and recovering my body,
Friday nights sometimes consist of me watching something
that will give me content ideas.
It's reflection of my week, goals I've accomplished, talking
to my mom,
She always finds a way to say something funny and we
crack jokes.

It's funny how as we get older, life becomes simpler,
It's the little things that make us happy and feel fulfilled.
The joy and happiness I feel spending time in nature brings
perspective to my life,
It's what I've longed for and now, it's become
a beautiful reality...

Jamell Crouthers

By K. S. Love
Username: kslove

A Perfect Day

An alarm-clock-free morning,
There's nothing more soothing.
I took my first sip of coffee
As I lounged by the window,
Absorbing the beauty of a day minus responsibilities.
"I love everything about today,"
I affirmed, consumed by my thoughts:

Maybe, I'll make the hour-long drive
To my favorite beach,
Visit a couple of discount stores,
Or stop by that cozy little restaurant, I adore,
For a savory meal and a delicious treat.

I could always search for
A binge-worthy show,
Grab a bottle of Chardonnay,
Pop some popcorn and snack,
Until I drift off into the most pleasant sleep,
Cultivating the sweetest dreams.

"You know what?"
I ask myself aimlessly...
"You're overthinking it...
The only way today will be perfect
Is if I do all of these things."
So, I did

K. S. Love

By Jane P.
Username: jpck918

Perfect Isn't Real

What is a perfect day? Well, in all honesty, there's no such thing. I could sit here and think about all the things that make life seem perfect. I'd rather not. That would make way for my mind to validate why other days aren't "perfect." Life is life. There's no way around it.

Perfect is undefinable, an opinion. An opinion I'm learning to stay away from after chasing it for most of my life. I've learned trying to be perfect and looking for perfection is a downhill spiral. I will never be truly happy in search of this. I've tried to be perfect in academics and sports, yet I've always been extremely hard on myself when I mess up. I've tried finding the perfect significant other, yet look for every reason why they aren't. I've tried to be perfect at my job, yet feel guilt when I can't do everything the exact way I wanted to. The list goes on.

But guess what? I am human! Humans aren't meant to be perfect. We are meant to fail and learn. We are meant to get embarrassed and be humbled. We are meant for rejection and leaning into introspection. Humans are meant to make a fool of themselves and change into the person they want to become. Nobody gets out of here perfect, and if someone acts as if they do, they've lost touch with reality.

I'm learning to be grateful for the small things. I'm learning to have hope when I feel like giving up. I'm learning life isn't all or nothing. I'm learning that giving my best is going to be different at times and that's okay. I don't need to wait until I feel things are perfect to take action. I take action, giving it my best effort that day, and there's nothing more I can do.

To be honest, I still feel I'm trying to find the perfect sentences, the perfect thoughts, to produce the perfect writing piece. But hey, I'm a human and still on my learning journey. Embracing truth within myself and the world and learning to be real is my new defined definition of what I thought I was searching for in perfection.

Jane P

By Michael Delianides
Username: madelianides

—————————

My Perfect Day
Oh Perfect Day

My perfect day oh perfect day
I feel like living my life my way
If I lose the joy of living my life
My reasonable happiness leaves me with my strife
I better be living this time of year
It don't matter if I shed a tear
If I'm not living happy or not
Forever in a web I shall be caught
My perfect day oh perfect day
My life shall go on I shall have no dismay
I want to live, that is my way
My perfect day oh perfect day

My perfect day oh perfect day
Life shall go on or so they say
I want to live for I am free
To do many things of value I see
I love to play music even swim
I don't care if my body is slim
I live my life breathing and glad
Glad I don't die, man that would be bad
I ain't afraid to be called up yonder
But it ain't my time yet so it I won't ponder
My life is mine I won't be swayed
My perfect day oh perfect day

Michael Delianides

By Ash Raymond James
Username: ashraymondjames

_____

An Ode To The Little Things

I stayed in bed
until I reached
the outskirts of morning.

The birds gave pep talks
instead of songs.

I got changed
and found ten dollars
in my pocket.

It's summer but it rained
and I wonder why nobody

has made laundry powder
that smells exactly like this.

I make the perfect eggs.

The toaster
that loves to burns the edges
leaves them edible.
I thank it for its kindness.

I go outside and jump in a puddle.
There is still that childhood dream
that it will be a portal
to an alternative dimension.
One where Netflix didn't cancel the OA.
One where we could trade
our sadness for money.
Gosh, would I be filthy rich.

Me and the neighbor
do our awkward dance.
The small talk jive.
We bow and say
'have a nice day!'
We really mean it.

I walk to the coffee shop
and the sky is still
rubbing sleep from its eyes.

The wind is playing solos
on telephone wires.

I hold the door for a stranger
and we share a smile.

I tell the barista a joke
and we both laugh
at how unfunny it is.

I take the ten dollars
and order a flat white, one sugar.
I say keep the change.

I find a bench, and I ruminate.

I realize
Happiness is right here —
why are we crying
like it is so far away?

Ash Raymond James

By Sofia Armstrong
Username: sofiagracearmstrong

Perfect Day

Hello my friend
May I share with you my perfect day?
I hope you'll stay until the very end.
First I wake with the golden sun, grateful and joyful—I pray.
Hydrate and fill this vessel with fuel
Moving and stretching keeps my emotions cool
Giving thanks for each moment I'm given
This life flows with grace like a ribbon
My love then goes freely to all of God's creatures
The large and small—all have different features
Life sweet like the slow drip of honey straight from the comb
I never rush, worry or stress because I know in my heart, I
am always home.

Sofia

By Bre Mcilroy
Username: brewithle

_____

Dear Father

In my perfect day
You'd still be here
We would be sipping coffee
By the pier
Watching the morning sunrise
Seeing the glimmer in your eyes

In my perfect day
We would read underneath palm trees
Taking in the ocean breeze
Snapping memories that will never leave

In my perfect day
Cancer wouldn't exist

Taking you away
Would be completely dismissed

In my perfect day
We would watch the sunset by the water
You would never leave
I'd still have my father

In my perfect day
I would live inside a world
Where there would be no fear
And when the day is done
You would still be here

Bre Lynn

By Gerald Washington
Username: lostone89

_____

A Perfect G.W. Day

Another day rises from the ground
But with a different flavor to it
A day of traveling and clearing the cluttered mind
And also creating a wonderful time

Let the special day start with eating some delicious breakfast
Food that speaks to my soul
That makes me feel whole
And inspires me to conquer the road

When the road and I meet
Some of my favorite songs and I greet
Like it's the first time

We're getting to know each other's mind
As I unwind during this special time

While jamming and cruising on an unknown highway
Various historical statues and beautiful land catch my eye
Giving me a positive high
That I don't want to end
But continue to ascend

And embrace this rare feeling
A beautiful beach awaits me
And hypnotizes my eyes
With its waves

It waves at me and says "come on in"
But, before I take my first jump
I just want to stare at its beauty
And take a million pictures of it

Then I charge to the calming water
Like a soldier ready to do battle
But only remain in the safety zone
While watching others enjoy themselves

The perfect ending to a perfect day
It would be great to have another perfect day tomorrow
If only this could become a reality.
For now, wishing and dreaming about it will surface

Sincerely,

Gerald

By Christina Wilder
Username: christina

_____

My Perfect Day

The perfect day for me is a day without pain
Because I go to sleep sad and I wake up insane
The perfect day for me is a day without stress
Because I walk around like I'm happy but deep down I'm
depressed
I smile to keep from crying I smile because it's all you can do
The perfect day for me is the day that I'm at peace with you
Amen

Christina Wilder

By Sun Rose

Backwards Through Perfect

What is a "perfect day"?

My head rested heavily on the pillow. Memories of the long
day swirled in my mind. Exhausted, but content from my
perfect day.
The empty tea mug was set gently in the dishwasher. My
book lay closed by my ruffled bed. Sleep was calling.
A movie left unfinished, the kitchen was clean. House reset
for another day.
The evening had been bustling with dinner preparations.
The counters dusted with flour, pans, and spices. The food
sizzled on the stove. Dessert wafted through the room.
Sunset called the evening home as we walked along the
water. My darling pup ran in ahead as the city lights danced

in the eyes of my lover.

The afternoon vanished from sight as pages were written, rewritten, and tossed. The book was being born.

Lunch was a quick salad break from a morning of creativity. Papers were strewn across the floor, books on the coffee table, and my favorite mug forgotten amongst the piles.

My typewriter pierced the air with the clatter of the keys ringing to remind me I was at a new line.

The late morning awakened my senses as I sat in a quiet coffee shop, mulling over plot lines, speaking commitments, and blog fantasies.

Breakfast was a moment of calm before the crazy, my mind released all emotion and thought as I journaled and planned my day. The pup dashed around the house, energetic from the morning run.

Water gushed from the faucet sputtering in protest from the shower head. I washed all sweat and worry away, hopeful for a new day.

The sun crept from behind buildings and slowly woke up from its sleep. I smiled, walking back from the gym. Another beautiful start to another beautiful day.

My mind woke up moments before I pulled myself out of bed, my lover squeezed my hand as I left for the gym.

What is a perfect day if not one spent doing what you love with who you love.

By Sun Rose

By Rachel Brennan
Username: rbren

Perfect Palette

Get out of bed
One leg after the other
Feel the sunshine
Thank you earth mother
Move my body
Energy rediscovered
Indulge in good food
Dopamine wonders
Learn something novel
A new lens uncovered
Protect my peace
If needed from others
Feel connected
With another

Rest and reflect
A time to uncover
Close my eyes and know
With love,
Today I colored

318

Rachel Brennan

By Lore X
Username: lorex

_____

I've Awoken

I've awoken
in cars
off a shoulder
overlooking the sea
started my day
with morphine
and coffee
and vomit on the street

I've awoken
in deserts
under one single tree
beside strangers
on carpets

slipped away quietly
I've driven til shadows
melt into sands
and the stars bleed
into purples and pinks
when cold weather
has dried out my hands
and I'm too hungover
to speak

I've awoken
in twin beds
in distant lands
with lillies draping my canopy
with no one around
to marvel at scenery
with me

I've awoken on grey days
a cold sweat
over spring
recalling the past without shame
without desires to go back
nor focus on summer
in the center
I'm growing between

throughout this wide world
all my wheel's quick rotations
all the planes
and the trains
and the rides
from London's Heathrow
to Grand Central Station
every dawn
I've awoken
to rise

every day is impeccable
all the struggles
and pain
so delectable
as the earth
flips through the slides
in my eyes a
projection of beauty
the greatest adventures
the perfect day
is the day
I'm alive
and I live it
and seize it—no matter the risk
perfection is this

what we all
wake up with
this wonderful gift
all scared and excited
to be welcome; invited

to live for the sake of living

to rise and to fall
to feel love and
feel lost
and the awe to awake—
awaken at all.

Love X

By Kevya Sims
Username: keyraw

Letter To Heaven

Our day starts with coffee — black, no sugar and two creams. Just how you like it. I would pour myself a cup too, even though I hate coffee, and sit both coffees on the end table by your rocking chair.

I can hear your voice now: "Thank you baby."

Your voice hoarse from years of labor. We would pick our cups up and sip at the same time. Well, not quite at the same time. I always forget to blow my drink first and burn my tongue. My face twisted up in pain. Whereas, you always blow your drink first and never take on more than you can bear. Literally and figuratively. Now that I am older, I admire how still you can be. Sitting, day after day, in the comfort of your rocking chair, drinking your coffee and watching Lifetime movies. I relish that stillness.

On my perfect day I will definitely have to be still. I wouldn't want to do anything at all, but put my feet up and drink bitter coffee. To some people the perfect day is a day on the beach, but any day spent being still with you would be perfect to me.

I get hungry about halfway through my cup. My stomach growls which prompts you to rock yourself out of your chair and head to the kitchen. Your walk weary from years of service on your feet. Following behind you, I grab a plate off of the table and hand it to you. You fill it with grits, sausage, eggs, french toast, a waffle and bacon. I could have made my plate, but you always made it for me.

"Just sit down at the table, baby. I got your plate," you'd say.

With an orange juice to match, I sit at the dining table and go to town. With a full belly, I waddle back to the love seat right next to your chair. I look outside and see kids playing, but I don't feel that pain in my stomach anymore. Growing up without someone to play with and share secrets with has always weighed heavy on me. I carried loneliness with me throughout my adolescent and teenage years —always an onlooker, a wallflower, the bullied. My perfect day I will not have those feelings or be consumed with looking to something that I don't have. Even though I didn't have a friend my age, I had a friend who didn't mind drinking coffee and watching movies with me on a random Saturday morning. You might have been fifty years older than me, but you were my best friend. You never turned me away and you always made me feel like I belonged. If I can have one more day spent with you, just being still, that would be the perfect day.

325

And I do have a secret to tell you, best friend. I miss you and I still hate coffee.

Kevya Sims

By Tamara Gallagher
Username: tgal

Simply Happy

Sleeping in until my heart is content
My kids, my kids, not throwing fits
No arguments please, it's what I need
Breakfast being brought to me in bed
The food is cooked perfectly
A coffee cup the size of my head
Carmel and hazelnut hits my nose
As I eat, I read my Bible
Soaking in His Holy fire
I climb out of bed
Brush my teeth
Take a long shower, soaking in the heat
Getting dress and going to a hair appointment
She does my hair exactly how I want

My feet and nails are next
Feeling relaxed from my head, hands and feet

We pack up the car to go have some fun
Heading to the beach to meet up with family
It's not just my kids and husband who's there
It's my family from my youth and His as well
We stay there all day, enjoying each other's presence
Time is flying by as we soak in the sunshine

Last minute plans are made
Deciding to go out to eat
Laughter and smiles and happy vibes
Hit our hearts as the day ticks by
We all embrace one another with a hug
Going home, the kids fall asleep in the car
Carrying them inside, tucking them in one by one

Now it's time for Mom and Dad
Alone time in our bed
Loving on one another in the present
Staying up as long as we can
Just cracking jokes, cuddling and watching our show
Until we fall asleep in one another's arms and hopes
Sealed with a kiss we end the day
With sweet dreams in peace

Tamara Gallagher

By Crystal Mulligan
Username: crystalmulligan

Done Differently

Unmasked
I have been creating perfect days my entire life
They weren't perfect for me
But what I thought perfect should be

I've been creating a life
One I thought I wanted
One I thought I was supposed to have

My perfect day would look like it does on TV
I have lived those days
Those days are not me

So many times I have had the perfect day
Shopping with the girls, brunch at a nice restaurant,
tanning by the pool
These things have left me drained, exhausted, confused

So many times I have created the perfect experience
To be let down
To not feel the way they seem

329

I've had my days
In comfy clothes, dim lights, friends each doing their
favorite thing
Cooking safe foods together, napping, making sure we're
hydrated
Watching things we've seen a million times; doing things
we've done a million and one
Laughing and giggling and crying and sitting in silence

I have left those days feeling so at peace
So rejuvenated
So myself

I have also left those days feeling wrong
It is not what being social is meant to look like
It doesn't match the script that is in my head

I am learning to live life
The one I didn't know that I wanted
The one that I am supposed to have

I will continue to create perfect days, for the rest of my life.
perfect for me.
I define what perfect should be.

Crystal Frances

By: Kelsea Guckin
Username kelsea

1,440 Minutes

My perfect day
could be fall or spring
at home or exploring
solitary or spent with the people who embody my joy.
There is nothing to be earned
no aesthetic to be achieved.
Perfect,
I am outside
connected with the earth
moving my body
in the ways that empower me.
I am cocooned at home
connected beyond the physical
using my creativity

in the ways that embolden me.
A perfect day
makes your soul swell
so mine,
I am in my body
I am in touch with all my parts
past present future
and my ties to everything around me.
My perfect day
I am at peace
with the beauty of my life
I am aware
of each moment as it comes and goes.
And now I know:
Perfection is in the eye of the beholder
and I behold perfection in abundance.

Kelsea Guckin

By Antoinette Gonzalez
Username: algonzalez

———————————

Childhood

Growing up on Sailor Moon
And looney toons
Slip and slides
Always with soapy eyes.
Carefree summers
We were Beach bummers
Adulthood far from our minds
Ice cream of many kinds
Manhunt and freeze tag
Always up for a good fart bomb gag.
Childhood was a bliss
Something you'll always miss.

Antoinette Lucila

By Vee
Username: lvwl094

A Perfect Day

A Perfect Day —

Is it something grand, that glistens in your eyes
Towering over the land
Or is it more miniscule

A moment that glimmers and refreshes your mind
A tiny tangent in the timeline that brings a surprise

They're all as grand or as granular as you'd like

At the end of the day, it's about how the passing of time
defines your mind

It's not repeatable in production—
But rather, something that is well worth casting

It's the small glances that you keep near
Let them shimmer
Let them steer.

That's my perfect day.

335

Vee

By Zinamene Emue
Username: zailee_writes

_____

A Regular Day

My morning started off calm
I awoke from the tweets
from the birds who were outside my window
perched up on a tree
I headed downstairs for a bite to eat
and I was greeted by my entire family
Mom's frying eggs and plantain
Dad's got a cup of tea
rest of my siblings are scrambling around the kitchen
doing their individual things
I pause for a moment
basking in the gratitude I feel for these scenes
later in the day I link up with the gang
which is always a treat

we headed down to the water
it was our favorite spot to meet
laughing about nothing
running amuck through the streets
the days I spent with them
I always felt the most free
by 6:00 pm the gang is itching to get into an activity
we go home
change clothes
and make our way to the roller rink
the dj is setting the tone
playing all the hottest beats
rolling with my entire crew
you'll fasho catch us rolling dirty
hitting crazy dance moves
giggling at the newbies who fall to their knees
at the end of the night we head to the water one more time
to chat about the things we seen
when we finally decide to part ways it was almost 3
I wish the days we spent like this last for eternity
being surrounded by no judgement
and love that comes with no fee
spending time with the people I love
is always a perfect day to me

Zemue

By Maggie Faye
Username: maggiefaye

The Perfect Day

My love and I wake in a new city.
Maybe a new country.

Either continental or café,
We enjoy a breakfast with good coffee
and pastries.
The chocolatiest of croissants,
The softest of scones,
and the warmest of waffles.

Then, we go for a walk.
We take our time to inhale the fresh air and
absorb the new city's noises and
admire its unique architecture.

Our walk ends at a bookstore.
As we wander the shop's aisles,
the bookstack we carry grows and grows and grows!
My love says, "Yes, of course we can buy them all."
(We are not worried about the logistics of getting the books home).
Once the stack is so high that
we can't see over it,
we buy them all.

On our walk back to wherever we're staying,
we make a pit stop for takeout.
Most likely Chinese food, but
could be Korean or Indian or poke, too.

Next, but before dinner, is a warm shower.
Rich instrumental music with dissonant harmonies
and bubbly shampoo.
Fragrance-free body lotion and French skincare,
Followed by the baggiest of sweatpants and
an oversized tee.

Now all squeaky clean, my love and I eat dinner
over a grand adventure on a screen.
All snuggled,
we fall asleep before the credits roll.

Maggie Faye

By Mz.EYG Queen Era
Username: mzeygqueenera

The Best Things In Life Are Free

What's my idea of a perfect day? Well, that's easy. I'm kind of more of a simple girl these days, now that I'm older. Actually, come to think of it, I never had the chance to really sit and think of what a perfect day would mean/look like for me from start to finish. Wow. I guess there really is a first time for everything. So here we go:

My Perfect & Peaceful Day.

As soon as I open my eyes, first thing I would do to get my day started is start with the prayer of the morning. Thanking our creator for another day is always a must do to reinsure a great start to a great day. I follow prayer with a meditation routine. That for me includes deep breaths while sitting in silence, journaling and reading—anything to help prepare me for the day. This centers my mind so that it's easier for me to be able to go out into the world and deal with those around me.

After maybe an hour or two, I would make me a nice snack or breakfast, which usually ends up being just a healthy quick snack because I don't really like breakfast. Then, I would do what I like to call a "self-care repair" routine. It's when I either take a nice bubble bath or a long shower with my favorite candles, music, and a book. It gives me more time to relax and enjoy my own company before heading out for the day.

After bathing/showering, I would go through my face-wash/skin routine as well. Then, after that, I'd put on my clothes and head out. If I'm not heading out then I would either read, or write a bit because I love writing (if you can't already tell lol), or listen to music and maybe watch movies for the remainder of the day.

If it's one of those days where I want to get some fresh air, I can always count on one of my favorite places: downtown at the lakefront or beach. Basically, anywhere with a big body of water. I love water. A nice walk on a trail is always a great way to get fresh air and become one with nature too. But it's just something about being near water, in water or just even being around water that soothes me. It calms me, gives me clarity and peace. I love it. I have been this way for as long as I can remember. Sometimes while sitting near the lake, I read or just sit and think. Sometimes I may even cry. But whenever I'm done, something about it always gets my creative juices flowing. Song lyrics or an idea to do a certain project may come to mind. So, nature and I work very well with one another. When I stop to appreciate her (nature), she does what she does, which is inspire.

Afterwards, I would go home, get started on those ideas and plans rigth away and start working towards accomplishing them. I always end my day with more mediation and prayer, being thankful for what that day has given me in preparation for a better tomorrow. Then, I'd take another bubble bath/hot shower, more self-care repair and relaxation to finish off the day before a night of great sleep.

I know, it may seem pretty boring to some, and that's okay. See, what I have learned as I have gotten older is that I value peace of mind and peace and quiet. Especially in today's world where peace seems hard to come by. So, sometimes you have to create your own peace. Prayer, Meditation, Fresh-Air, Nature and A Postive Mind-set all brings forth peace and creativity. And all of these things are 100% free.

mz.EYG

By Naiya Figueroa
Username: naiya123

———————————

This Day

The sun kissed my cheeks as I opened the blinds.
The silence echoed through the home,
Telling the tale of a good morning.

Warm on the inside and cold on the outside,
That's just how I like it.
It's the Earth's way of telling me to rest.
Although, this coffee is telling me not to be still,
I sat down, on my emerald green couch and focused on my
breath.

The comfort of my space is refreshing.
To know that I am my home has been nothing short of a
blessing.

How wonderful it is to dance in this love that has filled my
apartment.
Gratitude poured out of my mouth and onto my possessions.
This solitude allows me to exhale without stressing.

Self has made this place her home and she is here to stay.
Sitting in my sanctuary is what keeps me sane.
As the sun kissed my cheeks, it heard me say,
"This, my love, is a perfect day."

Naiya Figueroa

By Michelle
Username: shelle-belle

———————

Pain-Free.

Rise and shine you beautiful soul!
We have work to do today.
Roll that delicate body out of bed and awaken to the day of
wonders ahead.
Today feels like a good day. I Declare it, embrace it and give
thanks.
It's the perfect day to live.
I am embracing the relaxation and peace that has been
gifted to me on such a beautiful morning.
I stretch, and sit up, wiggling my toes as my legs hang down
from my bed. A giggle escapes my lips followed by a smile as
my dog mimics me. She nudges me and lets me know that it
is time to officially wake up.
I step off of my bed and stand tall. There's no pain at all. No

tingling, no burning, no stiffness at all.
I am at peace. I playfully ask my kitty Nirvana—"Do
I choose coffee, or green tea?" She meows back at me. I
dance around the the kitchen and I embrace being pain-
free. There is no stress or struggle as I start my daily chores.
You may think this sounds silly, the happiness that bending
down brings me as I slide on my shoes. I did it absolutely
pain-free and that is perfect. It's perfect for me.
The sun is shining so bright, and I put the leash on my dog.
Being pain-free has blessed me with a morning walk.
I have energy!
Enough energy to conquer the world, well, that is, enough
energy to conquer "My world" or, at least to conquer the
tasks that most days I am unable to. Today, I am pain-free,
and it is absolutely perfect.
I think it's a good day to go to the gym. Perfect day, that is.
I grab my bag, my book, headphones and my water bottle.
I'm a little bit nervous that this may not last, but quickly
push the thoughts away. As today, this moment I am pain-
free, and today is the perfect day.
My body moves freely, and with each breath that I take I
am breathing in love and gratitude. These days are few and
far between. Today, I woke up pain-free.
I am able to grocery shop without any fears or anxiety.
There is no looking over my shoulder. I am in the moment. I
am safe, and I am living life peacefully. Today, I give thanks
for walking up pain-free.
I am able to walk the three flights of stairs to visit my

grandmother. We're going to have lunch and play some games. Her company and her smile bring me so much comfort. I'm giving thanks for such a perfect day.
I woke up pain-free. I woke up with the chance to show the world the actual me. With a smile on my face, and my posture upright. I am filled with gratitude and peace. I am grateful for my life.
The perfect day for me, means living without pain. Without tears, and strain. Oh how I am grateful when I am blessed with a perfect pain-free day.

Shelle

347

By Karissa Howden
Username: karissahowden

_____

Free

I've never went to pastry school
But a baker I am,
Maybe one day, I'll add to the list-
homemade jam.
Working in my own kitchen while I raise and grow babies too,
I won't lie, never clocking into a serving shift wouldn't make
me feel blue.
An ideal day looks like this-
Coffee in the sunshine,
It's pure bliss.
Babies feed the chickens,
while mama works in the kitchen.
The yard is large;
With plants and gardens

It's easy to feel recharged.
Fresh foods and a bread business too.
Tired I'll be,
but I bet that's when I'll feel the most free.

Karissa Howden

349

By Sherry Noble
Username: sherno87

Find The Perfect

Dear Unsealers,

Sometimes it's fun to "make pretend," right? We all know there's no such thing as a perfect world, or a perfect person, or a perfect day even. For a moment here I am going to pretend that I can plan out a perfect day and tell you all about how it played out for me.

I woke up to the smell of bacon and eggs, and the sound of my cat purring softly in my left ear. To my right was an empty space where my husband normally lies, but he was in the kitchen making breakfast which is unusual for a weekday. I threw on some comfy clothes and made the bed. I hugged my husband from behind and thanked him for the delicious looking food I then enjoyed while watching the news as we always do. We decided to go take a walk in the nearby trail a few miles from our house, in our comfy clothes, and watch the tail end of the sunrise between the trees over the lake we were circling. No one was there because like I said, it was a weekday. I wasn't working this day. When we got back to the car we turned on my favorite song, drove around a bit, and stopped by a small local beach to take pictures. I love taking pictures at the beach! Soon it was lunchtime and we ordered sushi to go — my favorite. The perfect day was flying by, and I was enjoying every moment of it. We got home and ate our food, I took out my art supplies and painted a picture. Painting always makes me happy. Being home with my husband and cats makes me feel at peace. I LOVE daytime naps. So, on a perfect day, I obviously took a little nap. A perfect day wouldn't have to end, right? So did my perfect day ever end?

I'm here to tell you, every day may not be perfect, but you can find something perfect in every day. From that perfect day forward, I choose to look for the perfect part of every day. Oh, and I promise it won't always start with someone else cooking for me — I do enjoy cooking!

Sherry Noble

By Rick Writes
Username: rickwrites

Cloud 10

A silent thought that now demanded my attention.
The universe knew exactly how to reveal this to me.
A problem that I fixed had finally released me from its bind.
I was going home.
The road hugged my tires like excited friends reuniting,
Usually a 7 1/2 min walk, stretched to a 13-minute run.
13 minutes, the length of a how to video that I'm sure I'll be
frequenting more.
The garage door
creaked opened &
I was ushered inside.
The love of my life,
I husband to her Bride
her face full of:

fear,
wonder,
here,
follow me!
She exclaimed.
Every noise on the planet dissipated except our footsteps:
tile, carpet, tile.
The light switch felt like the weight of the world.
I found strength from your love to flip it.
A stranger awaited me in my own bathroom .
I was to confront this foe without any idea that my life had
found the meaning I was searching for
A vacuum of time,
my life In the rear view.
Thankful that I saw words,
instead of lines on that clearview.
But I only see one, where is the "not?"
What a terrible malfunction,
how could they have forgot?
Then, the beacon of truth
began to break through the mystery.
Those 8 letters have the chance to
alter history:
PREGNANT
Every emotion that I've ever felt became
unified-
all the pain of my adolescence,
all the courage of my youth,

all the fun of my independence,
all the worry of my work,
all the adoration for your mom,
They All joined together
to bring me this unmatchable joy.
The true essence of what it means to feel happiness,
I get to be a dad to a beautiful Baby Boy.

RW

By Jacqueline Sonia
Username: jsonia28

Broken Into Pieces

While grieving someone who is alive I slowly found myself and realized what I consider a perfect day.

I dated someone who broke me into pieces. He made me cry for days and nights, but I still loved him. I believe he lied to me constantly and made me overthink everything. I thought it was all love, but I was blind. Looking back, I believe I was manipulated into thinking he loved me. In reality, I think he loved himself. He made me feel small and I don't think he ever cared about my feelings. I fought for him and supported him. Everyone told me to walk away because they didn't think he would ever change, but I didn't believe them. I still stayed and thought to myself, 'he will change.' In the end, I finally realized what I thought was love was actually a lesson — a lesson that helped me to restore my true and happy self.

I learned from this relationship not to love easily. I learned not to trust people so quickly. And I certainly learned not to give someone multiple chances. When someone treats you poorly, walk away immediately. After leaving the relationship, I started writing again, and engaging in many other hobbies I have always loved. And I also feel so much less drained.

It wasn't easy to get to where I am today. I had to give myself time to heal and move on. There were so many days that I leaned on my friends. My friends watched me cry, and throw fits. They gave me advice, took me out on "friend dates," and stayed by my side during tough times.

I have since met someone who treats me well and makes me happy. Through the pain of losing a previous relationship, I learned the perfect day is one where you spend time with the people who bring out the best in you.

Jacqueline Sonia

By Rashan Speller
Username: artistphilly

_____

Rumination Of
The Sleeping Giant

Lips receding to the crease of stilled waters, underneath the bosom of the moon. The tide is forever in quivering forms. Yet there is beauty in the way the figures sit, a calm in the exciting exercise for life's sake. Time is forever in turning sails and moments constructed for the weathering of space and travel when harsh Squall perceived the deluged. Where are these inexhaustible Dispositions, these sounds to first utter the song of life. I want to hear this Song of Songs and Ballet to the grace of Ouayet caressing hymns. Listen as it wanders into the ears of man and whispers a prayer of Tolerance for the Middangeard yet harshly speak to the soul. Don't lie in your speech and yet don't comfort the weak. Be as you are and your voice shall sing in the tune of navigation until the sun reaches the moon. Siyabonga for

how I see you full and Siyabonga for how you return from
distant stars and a form I can love to learn. I hear the Song
of Songs and now I collapse to the weight of its existence,
this is the allure of your frequency and the power of your
youthful butterfly. May the sail cast shadow of your safe
returning to the Enterprise of a slight smile.

Rashan Speller

By Alexcia Cegelski
Username: alexcia23

_____

Family Party

I can recall a particularly bright summertime day
A big family party is held in the backyard
Everyone had gathered around from near and far to this event
The happy sensation of fits of laughter heard all around

A big family party is held in the backyard
I'm wearing my graduation cap and gown, and my high
school diploma is in my hand
The happy sensation of fits of cheer is heard all around
There is nothing but love that fills my heart

I'm wearing my graduation cap and gown, and my high
school diploma is in my hand
My elderly great-aunt came to me with a hug and a proud smile

There is nothing but love that fills my heart
I'm glad to have her here and see me graduate high school

My elderly great-aunt was close to me and had a proud smile
With a side hug, she smiled wide and posed with me
I'm glad to have her here and see me graduate high school
My mother begged us to take a family picture together

With a side hug, watching her smiling wide and posing with me
Other close family and friends wanted to pose with me too
As my mother begged us to take a family picture together
Before this excited, fulfilled party comes to an end

As other close family and friends wanted to pose with me too
Everyone had gathered around from near and far to this event
Before this excited, fulfilled party comes to an end
I can still recall this particularly bright summertime day

Alexcia Cegelski

By Lynn Humphreys
Username: lynn_bae

_____

Self-Care

I needed you all day
All day I yearned to climb up on you
Resting my face on you
Receiving all your warmth

You're the only one I allow to see me naked in daylight
You see me cry at night
You still hold me tight and let my tears soak into you

I'm self-centered but you're the only one I want constantly
I wake up to you and at the end of the day I gotta hurry
back to you

You're reliable like an old friend
You make me feel relaxed like a tall glass of red wine
You nourish me like a home-cooked meal
You're comfortable like hugs from mom
You're my sad goodbyes and my happy hellos

You are loyal. You would never abandon me. But where
would you go anyway?
You're just a BED. That's right. Furniture! This is a love
letter to my loving bed.
No further explanation. No other invitation. Also
my destination of Rest and Relaxation. Excuses of
procrastination.
Solitude acclimation.
Self-care affirmation.
A real staycation.
My own temptation.

B.E.D.
By End of Day....

You must Self care. Take care.

Aja Lynn Humphreys

By Dominic Valim
Username: itzheartfelt

Perfect Days My Way

There was never a perfect day for me.
Sure some were good or great. But I can't even imagine the
perfect date.

All the great days I ever had were so different. Sometimes
even looking back on them makes me sad. Like times had
with previous partners or friends.

I've come to realize even those days end. So did the
connections. Yet I'm still glad that they happened.

Without them I wouldn't be who I am today. Sure these
imperfections don't make things great, but there were
lessons learned along the way.

I think that is the important takeaway. To appreciate the time that you have. Making the most of each day. Even doing nothing has its grace.

Dominic Valim

By Destinee Ramos
Username: destinee

_____

The Perfect Day

Good morning
Draw the drapes
How can today be the perfect day?
A good day seemed days away
As I get up brush my teeth
I avoid eye contact with my reflection
Each time more bleak
Today will be different
I meet her gaze don't be afraid
Proclaiming you are not weak
If they cannot hear you when you talk
Makes sure they hear you when you speak
Take it easy there is no race
Yes you were betrayed

You and I escaped
We broke free from the shackles and the chains
This is your daily reminder you are safe
No remedy to ease the pain
The past you is slain
her death will not be in vain
The beauty of death's kiss
You can be reborn again and again
They have nothing to lose
You have everything to gain
The perfect day is being me
Not the victim he made

Destinee Ramos

By Poetry Veguez
Username: poetryveguez

_____

The Guilty Pleasures
Of Womanhood

I wish I could wake up in the morning
To a house that's prepped and made
No dishes or mess to clean up
The laundry is folded and put away

I wish that I was understood
That my efforts were noticed
And in return the context clues I love to scatter
Get swept up by loved ones
Offering to return the favor

I wish that I could walk the streets late at night
No mace or pepper spray in my line of sight
My keys are meant to unlock my door

Not clenched between my knuckles
Waiting to be bore

I wish that I could shake the hands
Of each passerby I encounter
Grinning widely from cheek to cheek
Exchanging pleasantries and
our hopes for the future
Morals aligning and feeling at ease
Knowing many people feel the same as me

I wish I had one perfect day
To rest and partake in hobbies
No work to stress
Just reading my favorite books in hotel lobbies
I would sing and dance and play in the rain
No anger left, no unresolved pain

Because womanhood is often a burden
That at times feels like a tyrant warden
Patiently waiting until my time is served
And knowing my aptitude is mildly absurd
But I often hope for the little things
Because to me they feel like extraordinary wins
And when this mindless duty is fulfilled
My perfect day will be without guilt

Poetry Veguez-Chang

By Kelly Lieberman
Username: kelly

_____

My Heart Is One That Desires Deep Human Connection. So My Perfect Day Would Look Something Like This...

I like to be quiet.

I like to get lost in the wrinkles that hug a stranger's eyes and wonder how much time he's spent in the sun. Did he live by the sea or get a chance to hold the hand of the one he loved under that same sun that embedded itself around his eyes?

I like to sit quietly in the loudness of a busy dirt road in a foreign land and make up life stories of those who walk by. How many scarves does she own and what made her choose the one with bold flowers and stripes and does she see herself as beautifully as I do? Did she tie up her hair and think, "damn I'm a queen" because she walks down this dirt road like royalty.

I bet she has scars in places no one can see.

Just like me.

I wonder if I pulled out my scars from their quiet place and shared them with her if she would pull hers out too.

And we could marvel at our human pain and laugh and eat food I've never heard of before.

And that man with the wrinkles around his eyes from a lifetime spent in the sun would walk up and hand us each a flower from his field and say something like, "All roses have thorns."

And when the sun begins to fall we'll put our scars back in their place and keep them safe for their next human embrace.

I'd thank her for her time and her smile and her humble beauty.

I'd let her know if she ever needs me I'll be here in quiet, making up life stories of those who walk by.

Kelly Lieberman

By Amanda Ann
Username: chatterboxinthemaking

————————————

Perfect Day

A Perfect Day is accepting there are no perfect days,
While there may be a flaw, a blemish upon the face,
There is the joy of lipstick,
A pop of color giving life to an old soul,
An iridescent smile accepting the stale reheated coffee, of which
Faded red lipstick stains still clutch on to old coffee mugs,
While the bittersweet memories remain intact,
An outlook has changed,
Despite being in bed tossing and turning the night before,
You spend your morning in gratitude,
Until you allow yourself to seize the day and run into life,
Allow yourself to not let your inner melodrama to bring
you down,
You inhale the air of life, and exhale the negativity,

A perfect day is not allowing the bad dreams in your body
To dictate your awakened state of reality,

I find the best moments in a perfect day to be full of laughter,
Laughter and having a sense of humor helps provide
sunlight
To a darkened room, I find that my perfect day is where
my sister
And I laugh and giggle like two partners in crime,
My perfect day is filled with moments of calm and piece,
It is not just a perfect day, but a days worth of memories,
That happily sit with me,
I find that there are perfect moments in the utter realms
of destruction,
Opportunities to make something broken stir alive again,

My perfect day is where I begin with a fresh mindset,
An early morning walk with the dog,
I allow my perfect day to not be a pity party,
But a day of forgiveness and healing,
A perfect day is flooding the darkness with pure light,
And not allowing the burnt stale coffee to foul my mood,

For in my perfect day I am freeing myself from what brings
me down.

ChatterBox

By Danielle Patino
Username: danimariexo8

_____

Beautiful Day

It's 6am
When the sun first
Wakes me — gently,
With caution,
As if a lover
Tiptoeing from bed
To brush his teeth
Before work,
A small light escaping
From under
The bathroom door;
I know I have no lover,
But I smile anyway —
I fall back asleep,

It is not yet
My time.

The sunlight nudges again
At half past 9, excited
This time — she wants
To spend her day with me —
The birds chirp to remind me
There is no rush —
I can keep resting
If I need to —
But I don't,
Not today.
I'll grab my novel
From my bedside,
Make pancakes and a latte
With maple syrup,
And sit
By the pool in the back.
Before lunch
I run a PR (personal record) at the track
Of the high school that
Broke me, but it won't
Break me today.
I'm stronger — I've trained —
And not
For weight loss, just
For me.

The clouds run with me
Around and around lane 3,
And I'm smiling to the
Sad songs on my playlist,
Immune—
I'm content enough
To stay smiling for now.

Dinner I do
With family;
Mom makes red sauce
From her garden tomatoes and
Dad makes salad
With oil and vinegar, and
My sisters
Are all home.
Mom tells a story about
The business she runs,
We tease her
Like we're children still,
And I go quiet while
They laugh.
Not a sad quiet—a
Museful one. I listen, awed;
It occurs to me I'll miss this
Soon.

I'm at the climax
Of the novel, I lounge
By the pool while
The sun is setting.
It becomes dark
And dad flicks on
The backyard lights.
The day's come
Full circle.

It's warm
But I hear mom's wind chimes;
There's fireworks
In the distance — someone's small
Celebration —
And I'm drinking peppermint tea
With milk. It's still only
9pm — my, I have hours
To keep reading.

At midnight I hop out
Of the shower, I throw a towel
Over my head.
I mark my novel finished
On Goodreads, I rate it
5 stars.
I wear a vintage bathrobe;
I know no one will see it

But it's enough
That I will.

I admire myself
In the full length mirror
And for a moment
It hurts
That I'm alone;
It's only for a second and
It almost feels nice—if
Only to remind me
Of all this good.

This beautiful world—
I watched a beautiful sunset,
I read a beautiful book,
I wear a beautiful bathrobe,
And I lay under my covers now
To write a beautiful
Poem.

Danielle Patino

By Dr. Cortnie S. Baity, LMFT
Username: onwardandupward

A Perfect Day

In a city I adore, the morning sun's kiss,
A perfect day unfolds, free of worry and pure bliss.

Awakening with gratitude, a heart full of grace. In God's
presence, I find my tranquil place.

A gym's vibrant energy or a fitness class so bright,
invigorating my body, an uplifting morning delight.

Professional goals embraced with an open heart and mind.
A purposeful journey, building dreams and maximizing time.

Shared some laughter and wisdom with a good friend.
These moments so dear. In her company, hope whispers,
dispelling loneliness and fear.

Through inspiring streets, I take a thoughtful stroll, a world-
class neighborhood, empowering my soul.

With a loyal puppy,
Abundance Love is her name, a playful bond, so sweet.

379

With her, there is never a dull moment, no emotional need
she cannot meet.

For me and the world, an abundance of love and joy she
spreads, she is so friendly, there is not a person or pup that
she has not already met in her head (lol).

As the hours of my day quickly march on,
it is afternoon already and much work has been done.

It is time for some well-deserved self-care. Perhaps I will
read a devotional and say a prayer or two, brief yet sincere.

I will remind myself that I worked hard to be here. I deserve
this. I belong.

Maybe I will listen to a good book or a few of my favorite songs.

I will end my perfect day with tasty dinner delights.
Perhaps, I will cook myself dinner, hmmm, I just might.

A feast for the senses, a culinary endeavor.
My home fills with aromatics of a meal I will savor.

380

As the sun sets, peace wraps its arms around me.
I'm so grateful for this day and night full of life, hope, and
serenity.

Sitting on my balcony, underneath the stars, I find a
tranquil reprieve, reflecting on the day. I am grateful: there
is still some good in this life for me, I believe.

Perfect in simplicity, this day I hold dear, thank you God for
this alignment. With God all things are possible.
With Him, whom shall I fear.

Dr. Cortnie S. Baity, LMFT

By Drew Zuhosky
Username: drew-zuhosky

_____

A Great Day

"Have a great day!" It's a common wish among friends and well-wishers. We can easily say to someone, "I hope that you have a great day today!" And, unlike other hopes that we might have, it is easy and effortless stuff.

At the core, it all depends upon what you make of your day. It has a different meaning for different people. Since we're here, I'll give you mine.

Simply put, my definition of a "great day" is easy as pie. A great day means getting up in the morning and being able to know that I have new episodes of podcasts to listen to in my feed.

Every weekday (barring major holidays), I start the day by listening to "Nothing Personal With David Samson." Samson is a former Survivor castaway and President of the Miami Marlins. He's smart, fresh, and funny.

A great day means that I can write. Since writing about combat sports is how I make my livelihood, I've had so many great days over the last six years.

Perhaps most importantly, a great day is one spent talking to and hanging out with the people most important to me. The greatest days happen when my nieces get to spend time with me, their uncle.

Thanks for reading. Make this day a great one.

Drew Zuhosky

By Lorinda Boyer
Username: lorinda

Perfectly Equal

Once upon a perfect day
All were equal in every way

Not color nor gender
Did prevent the render

Of kindness and care
Bestowed on everyone everywhere

In fact, all differences at hand
We celebrated in fashion most grand

And an impenetrable sphere
Protecting both straight and queer

And those dark skinned and light
Surrounded our earth, preventing a blight

Which threatened evil and strife
Upon this our most perfect life

For hate may have been the prequel
But equal would be the sequel

On this most perfect day
Conjured and imagined my way

Lorinda Boyer

Acknowledgments

Thank you to all our contributing writers who have bravely shared their truth to help change the world. One story, one poem, at a time, you all are making a difference.
Thank you!

If you would like
to read more
stories or write
your own, head to
TheUnsealed.com

Made in the USA
Columbia, SC
29 July 2024

39462641R00233